To
Hope you enjoy

FROM IN THE DUGOUT

The Real Deal about Baseball

Ronald "Ronnie" Smith

All rights reserved. No part of this book may be used or reproduced by any means, graphic, electronic, or mechanical, including photocopying, recording, taping, or by any information storage retrieval system, without the written permission of the publisher except in the case of brief quotations embodied in critical articles and reviews.

Table of Contents

Chapter 1: Making The Team 15

Chapter 2: Bitternesss A Dream Denied 45

Chapter 3: A New Beginning "Satchel Paige All-Stars" 51

Chapter 4: Time For A Change "The Atlanta Cardinals" 72

Chapter 5: Umpiring A New Gig 87

Chapter 6: Coaching A Living Legacy 98

Purpose

Most people who write books start out on their own with a desire to write and some idea of what they want to write about. This book is different. In all honesty, it never crossed my mind to write about my life while playing baseball. I lived every moment and all events are true, but I never thought of it as being important.

Writing wasn't a task I had considered doing until I reunited, through classmates.com, with a former high school classmate, Griselda Houseworth Clemons. She lives in Maryland and I live in Georgia. We talked often because both of us like to talk. Griselda was a teacher for forty-nine years and has this annoying habit (to me) of asking a lot of questions. It wasn't long before I began sharing stories about events that occurred and people I had met during my extensive baseball career. She always wanted to hear more and more. It's a good thing she's a good listener since one story would lead to another and another and then another. I have lived with all these experiences, stored in the recesses of my memory, but never shared them with anyone; not even my family. She was astonished by the sheer volume of experiences I had had in the fifty years since we had last seen each other. I amazed myself.

Once the floodgates opened, each story took on a life of its own. I want to thank Griselda Houseworth Clemons for being so patient and understanding each time I called to share another remembrance. It wasn't long before she suggested that I tie all my stories together and put them into a book. Her words were, "I can see myself reading this book and I don't even like baseball." She described the stories as interesting, unbelievable, fascinating, humorous, entertaining and even educational. Her interest caused me to pause and go hmmmmm, I'll think about it. Griselda began her campaign to get me to record my stories in the early spring of 2013.

She never let me forget. She asked me about my legacy to my family. She called me selfish for not wanting to share my history with them. She countered with, "This is their family history, too and they need to know this." She didn't play fair. Griselda knows how much I love my family. She insisted that they needed to be made aware of my struggles as well as my triumphs throughout my baseball career. She constantly reminded me of my participation and contributions to the tomes and annals of baseball history. She asked the question, "Why should they hear about your exploits from others, after you die, when they can hear about them directly from you while you're still living?" One statement she made struck a chord and stayed with me: "As African Americans, it is not only our responsibility to pass down the family history from generation to generation so that it doesn't get lost, it is our duty."

The realization came slowly that I am a part of baseball history. I had never thought of myself in that light. True, I played for the Atlanta Cardinals after a brief stint with The San Francisco Giants. True, I played alongside the great Satchel Paige. Yes, I played in the Baseball Negro League. When I looked at the written word, there was no denying I, Ronald MacArthur Smith, am definitely a part of the history of baseball.

During my baseball career, I was a player, a coach, an umpire, a recruiter and now retired. There were stories on top of stories associated with each stage of my life.

I finally felt confident that I had a book, maybe two or three to write. To encourage me, Griselda offered to help. After about six months of avoiding the subject of writing, I finally decided to try. I e-mailed my first segment, how I made the high school baseball team, to her. She edited it and sent it back to me. I was surprised by my reaction to seeing my words come to life. The edited version sounded terrific when I read it. We continued this process until the final page was completed. So, I offer my sincere thanks to Griselda Houseworth Clemons for encouraging, motivating and gently persuading me to do this. I hope you have as much fun reading, **From in the Dugout: The Real Deal about Baseball** as we had writing it.

Ron Smith

Baseball: The Real Deal

A Baseball Family

I guess it would be safe to say that I have a baseball family. I never met my maternal grandfather but I was told he was a good baseball player. My younger brother, Arthur Neal (Ricky), always loved the game of baseball. He started going to *The Braves* stadium so much that he eventually secured a job there. At the impressionable age of 12 he was one of the first Black ball-boys for *The Braves*.

Rickey played baseball in high school. He was such an exceptional hitter that he landed a baseball scholarship to *Morehouse College, an HBCU.* * He was spotted by a scout and later signed to play professionally with *The Atlanta Braves.* This had always been his dream. After his playing days ended, he later became a Scout for The Braves.

My name sake, my son, Ron Smith Jr. chose to play the game of baseball at an early age and continued all through high school. I enjoyed coaching my son while he played Little League Baseball. He had the gift of making difficult plays look easy. He was the type of player every coach dreams of having. This kid paid attention. He followed directions. He was cooperative and he practiced without being told to practice. I'm not saying this because he's my son. I'm saying this because it's true. After graduating from high school, he accepted a full baseball scholarship to *Southern University, an HBCU*.* A Scout for *The Chicago Cubs* saw him and the rest is history. My son signed with *The Cubs* and went on to play professional ball. He now puts all his energy into his son, my grandson, who is also a natural baseball player.

Chad Smith, my grandson, plays with *South Gwinnett High School* in Snellville, *Georgia.* This is his junior year, 2013-2014. He has already committed to *The*

University of Georgia (UGA) to play baseball when he graduates in 2015. Several major league scouts have attended his games to get a better look at him. A few have even made contact. He is a phenomenal player who can play more than one position and play each one equally as well. The summer of 2013 was exciting and exhausting for him and his father. He appeared in numerous showcases. He was seen in Chicago, Florida, California, North Carolina, Dallas, Texas, Georgia, Minnesota, New York and Louisiana. Remember the name, Chad Smith.

My brother, my son and I look at this kid in amazement. He is so skilled and proficient for his age. He makes decisions on the field like an adult, not a fifteen year old. The three of us have agreed that he has inherited the best from each of us which makes him a superior player. He is also very bright. Chad stays on the honor roll. He gets that from his daddy. Remember the name, Chad Smith.

***HBCU: Historically Black College/University**

A DYNAMIC BASEBALL FAMILY

RONALD "RONNIE" SMITH

PATRIACH

PAST

PRESENT

FUTURE

A DYNAMIC BASEBALL FAMILY

ARTHUR

NEAL

Chad Smith

BASEBALL, THE REAL DEAL FROM THE DUGOUT

By

Ronald "Ron" Smith

Griselda H. Clemons, Co-writer

CHAPTER 1

MAKING THE TEAM

Making The Team: Young Ronnie (12–14 Yrs. Old)

"PLAY BALL" are the two most exciting and energizing words in the English language. My heartbeat quickens when I hear those words. My eyes light up like Fourth of July fireworks. My legs feel charged and ready to take off. That's the thrill of baseball. As a young kid, I grew up in Rockdale a neighborhood outside the city limits of Atlanta, Georgia.

I loved baseball and played every chance I got. Organized sports, like Little League Baseball and Pee Wee Football, were for Whites only. It didn't bother us, in the Black neighborhoods, that we didn't have equipment. We were accustomed to either doing without or accepting the second-hand items from the white schools, recreation centers, sports organization, etc.

When they got new anything, we received their old whatever. This arrangement taught us to be creative and resilient. If we didn't have a baseball, a tennis ball would do. If we didn't have a bat, we used anything with a solid handle from the house or the backyard; broom, mop, ax, hoe, rake, etc. Our parents were mad as hell when they discovered their tools with missing handles. They couldn't understand why these items kept breaking.

When they discovered what was happening, we didn't care. We were willing to suffer the consequence. We had to play baseball and we needed something to play with. When we let the girls play, they used a plank of wood since it was wider. I remember playing baseball in parking lots, the street or a vacant lot. Traffic had to stop and wait for us when we played in the street especially if we were in the middle of a play. In other neighborhoods, those kids were fortunate enough to play in city parks.

I first started playing in the 18 and Under League established by the city of Atlanta's recreation department. I was twelve years old. My natural talent for this game evolved quickly. I was able to run, hit, throw, field and anything else that was asked for. Some said I was a fine-tuned player. Looking back, I guess you could say, I was a pretty good ballplayer.

Most of the 18 and Under League games were played at Anderson Park. All parks closed at 10:00 PM. Mr.

Ralph Long was the administrator of the park. He knew when the lights were going to go out so he would come to the field and announce,

"You got 15 minutes." We continued playing.

"You got 10 minutes." We still didn't stop playing. "You got 5 minutes."

And before we knew it, all the lights in the park would go out which left us fumbling around in the dark. We didn't realize the lights were on a timer operated by the city of Atlanta. As kids, we thought Mr. Long was the meanest man alive because he turned the lights out on us and wouldn't let us finish our game.

At the age of 14, I entered the brand-new Samuel Howard Archer High School. It was the fall of 1956. I was in the 9th grade. As the sports departments were getting established, it was only natural for me to try out for Archer's first baseball team.

The coach split everybody who came to try out into two teams to play a practice game. I was placed on a team against Richard Andrews, one of Atlanta's top pitchers. I was the only one to get a base hit for my team in that game. We were showcasing our skills for a place on the varsity team. Coach picked his team. I didn't make it.

The 'B' team was next; after all, I was only a freshman and freshmen don't usually make the varsity anyway. I didn't make the "B" team either. I didn't understand what was going on. I thought something must have been wrong with Coach's eyesight. Why didn't he recognize my skills? Didn't he see how much heart and enthusiasm I had for the game? Since the roster was on the wall, a friend of mine, Eugene Anderson, added my name at the bottom of the list. The rest is history. Not once did I have to say, "Put me in Coach!"

During the time of the segregated South, Black schools did not receive the same materials, supplies and equipment as the white schools. That was the case at my new school Archer High. None of the sports teams had uniforms. The band didn't have uniforms either.

Other schools laughed at our baseball team and teased us because our uniform consisted of baseball caps and white 'T' shirts. When the team got ready to play its first game, coach transported his team in his old beat up station wagon. Even though my name wasn't officially on the roster, Eugene, my friend who added my name,

told me to get in the station wagon with the rest of the team. That's what I did. I'll never forget what happened at that game.

Making The Team

Let me give a little background information about the sport of baseball for Blacks in Atlanta. Black schools didn't have baseball diamonds. They had football fields and basketball courts but no diamonds. We had to play at different recreation parks around the city of Atlanta. My new school, Archer High played its first game at Anderson Park which was located across the street from Turner High, my former high school. About the 5th or 6th inning, we were losing but the bases were loaded. Coach said,

"I need a pinch hitter."

Eugene Anderson pointed at me and said, "Let him hit coach."

You see, Eugene and I played on the same neighborhood team and he knew my strengths. For some reason, Coach respected Eugene's knowledge of the players because he pointed at me and said,

"Go ahead son. Get a bat and get up there."

Since I wasn't officially on the roster, I didn't have a cap. I got Eugene's cap and took my position. I remember thinking; this is what I was meant to do. I got a single and we scored two runs. We won the game and I started the rest of the season. The next year, my sophomore year, I made the Varsity. My position was right field and I batted over 400 the next two years. I don't claim responsibility for the success of our team because this was a great combination of players. Our team was loaded with players who had natural born talent. We won the next two city championships. We were proud of our efforts. We, the first baseball team at Archer High, placed the first two trophies in the school's trophy case.

During my junior year at Archer, 1958 - 1959, I played during the summer with a newly formed team called the Rockdale Rawhides of the Georgia/ Alabama league. That is when I met Charlie Davis who had played with the Memphis Red Sox in the Negro League. We had a great team made up of mostly high school players. I was placed in the starting lineup and played two seasons with that team. In a play-off against Montgomery Alabama, I hit three home runs in one game.

Graduation and The San Francisco Giants

After graduating from Archer in 1960, I heard tryouts for the San Francisco Giants were being held in Marietta, GA that summer. This was my chance to see if I was as good as people said I was. I went and did well on the first day. I hit a single, a double, a triple, and a home run. I felt good about my performance but I didn't know how the Giants' scouts felt about my performance. I never did complete my tryout. They stopped me in the middle of tryouts, telling me to go home. I couldn't imagine what I had done wrong. So many questions were swirling in my head. What could I have done better? What were they looking for? Why did they stop me? I needn't have worried because that weekend Dale Alexander, one of their scouts came knocking at my door with a contract offer. My grandmother gave me her blessing which made that the happiest moment of my life. Can you imagine how a boy, a Black boy, not quite 18 years old felt? This was the opportunity of a life time. I hurried up and signed that contract. I didn't ask any questions about salary, benefits or anything else. I was going to play baseball and that was all that mattered to me.

A few of my friends were getting married. Some were preparing to go to college. Others didn't know what they were going to do. However, I, Ronald MacArthur Smith, was packing my bags getting ready to leave home for the first time. At the age of 18, I was going all the way from Rockdale, Georgia to Casa Grande, Arkansas for spring training. I was looking forward to realizing my dream. I was scared but happy.

Traveling to Quincy, Illinois: 1st Stop; Waco, Texas

"We don't serve Niggers here!"

After leaving spring training in 1961, the team headed to Quincy, Illinois by bus. Our team was a diverse team; a couple of black players, a few Cuban players and many White players. We had been on the road for a long time and decided to stop at a restaurant in Waco, Texas. We were hungry and ready to chow down. All of us went in together, sat down and picked up the menu to see what was available. While looking over the menu, the waitress came over to the table where I was sitting and addressed me. I didn't know why she chose me, but she said,

"We don't serve your kind in here."

I didn't immediately understand where she was going with that. I was just a hungry man, traveling with my team; not thinking about being in Texas and segregation laws. So I said to her, very politely,

"Well mam, I haven't ordered anything yet." She then said in a very strong voice,

"We don't serve Niggers in here."

I was stunned by her remark. I sat there for a moment, trying to compose myself because I wanted to tell her, "That's good because I don't eat them. They don't digest well." Needless to say, I didn't because I didn't want to spend any jail time in Texas. All of the black and Cuban players got up, without saying a word, and went back to the bus without eating anything. Jim Thrower, a teammate, came out to the bus and offered to bring us some food. I turned his offer down because I was too embarrassed and angry to eat. I grew up in the South. I knew what the laws were about keeping blacks and whites separated. I was forced to remember that while Texas is located in the West, it is also the Southwest portion of the United States. We were anxious to leave Waco, Texas and continue on our way to Quincy, Illinois.

Traveling to Quincy, Illinois: 2nd Stop, Kansas City, Missouri.

"Get up! Get up! Don't sit by me!"

We made one more stop in Kansas City, Missouri. This time, we went to the bus station's waiting room. This was a large area with very long benches arranged like church pews. To my eyes, they appeared to be at least 20 feet long. They probably weren't but that's how long they seemed to be. I was so tired after playing and traveling all in one day. I noticed a White lady sitting at the other end of one of these butt and back killers. Her presence meant nothing to me since she was so far away. As I started to sit on the other end of the same bench she was seated on, she started screaming from the top of her voice,

"Get up! Get up! Don't sit by me."

People stopped what they were doing to look at what was causing this commotion. You would have thought I had committed a crime. I learned that in Kansas City, it is against the law to sit on a long bench occupied by a white person, even though you're at the other end. I got up and left the waiting room so that foolish woman would shut up and I could cool down. It was beginning to hit me that racism existed in places other than Georgia. It was a relief to leave those places behind where people of color were not welcome. Being on the road like that was an education.

Quincy, Illinois

We finally arrived in Quincy, Illinois without any more mishaps. After all the Black and Cuban players had been through, we couldn't believe we were going to be able to stay in the same hotel as the White players. After all, it was only 1961.

Things went well in Quincy for a little while because the baseball season hadn't started yet. Our routine was to work out every day and go out clubbing and/or bar hopping every night. That was a way of life for baseball players in those days. I don't see where too much has changed today. I met a White girl from Florida. She liked to hang around black men. We became good friends but nothing else. We met every night at the bar and had fun. She was a big drinker and set out to prove it every night.

One night, I decided to leave the bar early and go back to the hotel where I was staying at the time. My good drinking buddy decided that she would come to my room, uninvited, and surprise me. She went to the hotel and asked the desk clerk for my room number. My manager, Buddy Kerr, was in the lobby at the time and overheard her ask for my room number. He followed her up to my room and waited while she knocked on the door. She had no idea she was being followed. The knock surprised me since I wasn't expecting anyone. My first reaction was to ask myself, what in the world is she doing here. I really didn't want to be bothered but I let her in. My manager revealed himself and came in behind her.

"What the hell," I thought. "Is this woman setting me up? What's going on?"

Buddy didn't waste any time. He immediately began cursing at me and saying things like,

"What is she here for? This ain't no damn picnic. You're not here to be screwing around. You're here to play ball and don't you forget it. This is a damn business."

I was pissed off because I had done nothing to deserve his wrath. What was he so mad about? It wasn't even past my curfew. My, no longer friend from the bar, with her drunk ass, was sitting in the chair crying, talking about how sorry she was. She didn't mean to get me into trouble. I didn't even make a comment to her or to Buddy. I always felt he was a racist. I just simply said,

"yes sir."

I knew my place. I also knew we didn't like each other. However, I was not going to do anything to jeopardize my position on the team. As soon as he left, I didn't waste any time putting this drunk out of my room. I told her, through clenched teeth, not to ever come to my room without being asked. I slammed the door behind her as soon as she stepped over the door sill, letting her know I was serious.

Eating and Sleeping in Salem, Virginia

A few weeks after that incident, I was called into Buddy Kerr's office to receive the team's new assignment which was Salem, Virginia. Salem is near Roanoke, Virginia just like Atlanta is near Decatur, Georgia. Fred Moten and I, the only Blacks on the team, and the three or four other players from the islands packed our bags while making preparations to go to Virginia. We knew the drill by now.

Once we got to Virginia, we noticed the living arrangements were vastly different from those in Quincy, Illinois.

The Giants had made arrangements for the white players to be sent to a hotel downtown. The rest of us were sent across the railroad tracks to live with black families. This too, had been prearranged by the Giants. The living conditions weren't bad at all. The people had vegetable gardens in their back yard. Since they cooked for us, too, we were guaranteed fresh vegetables every day. We ate much better than the guys staying in the hotel.

However, I often wondered why all of us couldn't stay together and be together as a team just as we were in spring training, on the field playing and also living together in Quincy, Illinois. We always had to separate when we traveled and/or played in the South. That was the law of segregation. "When in Rome…………" However, my young mind wanted it to be different.

We traveled by bus whenever we had a game in a nearby town.

To this day, I have a hard time believing how it became my job, when we were in these southern towns and cities, to take the guys of color to find somewhere to eat after the night games. It was also my responsibility to insure the safe return of the colored team members back to the bus at a later time.

When on the road, we, the colored players, knew the greyhound bus station had a section where we could eat or we looked for a mom and pop restaurant/carry-out somewhere. Keep in mind, the Giants always stressed to us to eat good each day. To insure this, we were allotted meal money which was approximately $6.00 a day. In those days, a meal only cost about $1.00 and change. A hamburger was about twenty cents.

If you've ever traveled by bus, you know that the bus station is not the best place to eat if you need to eat well. However, we had no choice. Our White teammates did not have a problem eating well since they could eat in the hotel or any restaurant of their choice.

On to Belmont, North Carolina: Racial Tension

"Nigger, take your black ass back to Georgia."

After about a month in Salem, I was called into the office again to receive my assignment. I was going to Belmont, North Carolina to play in the Western Carolina League. Management stressed that Blacks had never played in Belmont before; so, we had to look out for, avoid, and not cause any racial situations. We were advised to ignore racial slurs and be on our best behavior at all times. After arriving in Belmont, we were introduced to the family we were going to be living with; just like in Salem. We started out playing a game every night. We played a couple of games without any problems.

This caused us to relax and let our guard down. Then it happened. I remember like it was yesterday. I was at bat. I hit the ball and ran to first base. The umpire called me out. I thought I was safe so I disputed the ump's call. In the middle of the dispute, I heard this voice coming from the stands yelling,

"Nigger take your black ass back to Georgia."

Let me explain. When you purchased a ticket to the ball game, you received a program that listed each player's name, age, and place he was from. That's how the guy yelling knew I was from Georgia. I was already angry with the umpire and now this. I made a few steps towards the stupid fan but stopped myself. I was more hurt than mad. I had to remind myself to calm down and not lose my temper. By this time, I was just tired of being the recipient of all this racial abuse.

That night I called my mother and told her that I couldn't take it and I was leaving and coming home. Since she had always worked for white people, she understood what I was talking about. She told me I'd better not give up and quit. She reminded me that Jackie Robinson had gone through much worse and he didn't quit. She stressed the point of how he had paved the way so that I could have this opportunity that I'd decided to throw away. In her angriest tone, she told me that I may as well spit on all he had achieved for my skinny ass.

By the time she finished, I was no longer angry at the ump or the fan yelling from the stands. It was my time to do my part to continue paving the way for other young Black boys who wanted to play in the professional sport of baseball. My mother told me I had to tough it out. So, I unpacked my suitcase and stayed even though, at the time, it got no better.

The Corner Store

"Here Come a Nigger"

One morning, while out walking, trying to get acquainted with the neighborhood, I noticed this little corner store which reminded me of home. I decided to check it out. As I entered the store, a bell rang, just like at home. This made me smile.

When I got into the store, I heard,

"Here come a nigger, here come a nigger."

That's when I noticed the parrot, sitting on his little trapeze swing bar, looking at me through the bars of his cage. I thought to myself, I can't even catch a break away from the baseball field. Someone has even trained a damn bird to call me a nigger.

I watched the owner as he came hurriedly from the back of the store. He appeared to be a little flustered. After I had made my selections and placed them on the counter, we began to talk about so many things. He turned out to be a very nice person.

However, I never forgot, not for one second, that he was the one who had taught his parrot that greeting. I guess he felt guilty about it since he often didn't let me pay for my items. I visited his store regularly since it was like a small general store, more like an early dollar store with wearing apparel. Believe it or not, I enjoyed my conversations with the owner. I just hated his bird.

The Invisible Center Fielder at the Beauty Contest

After a few weeks in Belmont, I was given some tickets to distribute in the Black community in hopes of encouraging more black people to come to the games. During those early days of Minor League baseball, there was a section for whites and a section for Blacks just like everywhere else in the South. Schools, churches, restaurants, buses, trains, bathrooms, water fountains, movies, bars, neighborhoods, etc. were supposed to be separate but equal. That looks good on paper but not true in reality.

Black fans sat out in right field away from the white fans. It was hard to get Blacks to come to the games because they didn't want to sit so far away from the action. That's the reason why I didn't even make an effort to give the tickets away or try to get anyone to come. I wasn't aware of the plans to have a beauty contest as entertainment before one of the games.

The night of the contest, it was announced that each contestant would be escorted by members of the starting lineup. I was the only Black player in the starting nine at the time and I KNEW I was not going to be allowed to escort one of those White girls anywhere. That's when my slow brain caught up with what was happening. They had needed a Black girl for me to escort. Oh well! I messed that up by not distributing those tickets.

Moving right along, the beauty contest started. It began with the catcher escorting the first young lady. Next, the pitcher was called. After him was the first baseman, then the second baseman, next the shortstop, after him, the third baseman. The suspense was building because the crowd was sitting on the edge of their seats watching and waiting. They knew the order of the lineup of the top nine and my name would be called soon since I played center field. The announcer called for the left fielder. The stadium became very quiet at this point. Guess who was supposed to be next? That's right, the center fielder which was me. When the announcer called for the right fielder, you could hear a sigh of relief. Some applauded. Others laughed. That was hard for me to take but, I left the field and went back into the clubhouse until they finished. For some reason my name had not been called to escort a girl. I wondered why they did that. They had skipped right over the center fielder as though that position didn't exist. Maybe they forgot the center field position.

I thought up every excuse in the book for that blatant oversight. No one from management said anything like we're sorry that we had to do that or anything else. They acted as if it didn't happen.

The silence from my teammates said it all. Everybody knew, even me, that a Black boy/man was not going to be allowed to escort a White girl/lady anywhere in

North Carolina. I was angry because I had been humiliated in front of all those people. Management could have explained before the game that I wasn't going to be included in the lineup for the fashion show. I wasn't born yesterday. I would have understood.

Know Your Place

Growing up in the outskirts of Atlanta, I had been taught my place, as a Black man, in society. I knew where to go and what to expect when I got there. My grandmother, my great-grandmother, my grandfather, my aunts and uncles were always there to lead me, guide me and protect me.

They were also there to explain the rules and laws of segregation. I really needed them now. I was raised to view myself as somebody with a bright future ahead of me. I was a winner, not a loser. At my age, it was difficult for me to comprehend what was happening all around me. I had not been exposed to racial prejudice in this form.

I knew it existed but it had never happened to me, personally. I knew where I could and couldn't go. I knew what I could and couldn't do. I knew where I could and couldn't live.

I knew my place and I stayed there. Traveling with the Giant's baseball team made me grow up faster than I wanted to. If I wanted to survive, I had to learn fast what was expected of me on the road and in all the states. The road I traveled was not an easy one. There were bumps and gravel; potholes and cracks, sometimes trash; straight and crooked lines, curves and detours. I was coming into my own at this time.

I began to question the philosophy of segregation. It didn't make sense to me. My question wasn't "Why?" but "Why not?" This thought was gaining momentum across the nation in Black communities, especially with the younger generation. Young people wanted equal rights. I just wanted to play baseball. However, that came with a price. I had to become a hitting robot. I was supposed to ignore the cruelty and vulgarity of the fans and other players as well. I was not to lose my temper. The ump was always right. I was to obey my manager. I was to become an unfeeling, boring, non-thinking human being. I didn't think so!

Ending the Season in Belmont

By this time, I had had enough. I was waiting impatiently for this season to end. I believe our last game was played in Statesville, N.C. I don't even remember the score. After the game, we packed our equipment and headed for the bus to take us back to Belmont. At the last minute, I decided to ride back with the manager Max Lanier and three other players in his car.

On the way back to Belmont, we wanted to get something to eat so we stopped at a restaurant in a little town called Gastonia. Max and the other players, all white, got out of the car. I was the last to get out. He opened the trunk of his car and offered us a beer. That was part of my reason for riding back with Max because he always traveled with a cooler filled with beer. I was thirsty and in need of a cold one after the game. The offer was made and I accepted. They went inside and I remained outside since I knew my place and my place as a Black man in Gastonia, North Carolina was not in this White restaurant.

To pass the time away, I went to the phone booth to place a call home to a girlfriend. What happened next was like an adventure lifted straight from a movie. While making the phone call, I saw two policemen approaching the phone booth. I hung up immediately.

I was anxious to see what they wanted. They spoke to me and asked what I was drinking. I told them I was drinking a beer. One of the officers took it out of my hand and poured it on the ground. I'm staring at this officer, wondering what this was all about. Then the officer asked a peculiar question.

"Don't you know this is a dry county?"

A dry county? Hell, I had no idea what a dry county was, so I answered, "No sir." When he said,

"Okay, come with us, you're under arrest."

No Black man likes to hear those words especially in the South. My heart skipped a beat. Under arrest, what in the world did I do that warranted me being arrested? That's what I thought, not what I said. I asked if I could go inside and tell my friends. The answer was an emphatic no. I tried explaining to them that I was a baseball player and my manager was inside. They were deaf to anything I had to say. They said sorry, let's go. I was placed in the back of the police car and we headed toward the jail. This gave me time to think about my situation. I couldn't help but wonder why they didn't handcuff me and what they were going to do to me.

It was quiet inside the car until a domestic violence call came through the radio. Instead of continuing on to the jail, they headed to the fight. Remember, I'm still in the car. We went way back into the woods, where there was nothing but trees; no lights, no nothing. I knew what white cops did to black men when no one was looking as in, no witnesses. That's when I began to really get scared. All kinds of thoughts started floating through my mind. There I was, a lone Black man, out there in the woods with the police and nobody, I mean nobody, knew my whereabouts. My first thought was, maybe they will beat me to death and leave me out there in the woods. No one would ever find my body. I was scared as hell. It's a wonder I didn't crap my pants.

We finally got to the place where the call originated only to find this little old drunk man and his wife outside still fighting. The policemen got out and called the man by name. The couple stopped fighting immediately. One of the officers called the man to come over by the car. He talked to him and told him to go into the house. He asked the woman if she was okay. She said she wasn't hurt. He told her to go back inside and don't call them anymore that night. That, was it? They only got a talking to? I was amazed. If that had been in my neighborhood, everybody would have been handcuffed and taken to jail.

It was with a sense of relief when the officers returned to the car. I have never prayed so hard in my life as I did when asking God to let these officers take me to jail. At that moment, I wanted to go to jail more than anything in the world. Fear of the unknown was still with me because we were still deep in those dark woods. One of the officers broke the silence by asking me where I was from. I told him Atlanta but by Grandmother was from Griffin, Georgia. He replied,

"Griffin, Georgia, that's where I'm from."

Next, he asked if I knew the Turnipseed family. I answered, "Yes, they're related to my grandmother."

"No kidding, I know them well," he said.

After that exchange, the officers appeared to relax and became a little nicer. I relaxed, too. That's when I felt a shift in the atmosphere inside the car. I was no longer in fear of losing my life.

When the car pulled up and parked in front of a residence, the driver stated, "We're here."

I thought, Here? Here, where? I didn't see anything that looked like a jail. This was evidently the house where the sheriff lived. "Why are we stopping at the sheriff's house?" I asked myself. We went inside.

As I looked around, I noticed some stairs and there at the top of the staircase was a jail cell. I couldn't believe my eyes. However, they never took me upstairs.

In fact, I was led into the office and told to have a seat. One of the officers let me use the phone.

The only person I wanted to call was Max Lanier, my manager. Cell phones hadn't been invented yet. I imagined he must have been worried about my disappearance. When he came to get me, he couldn't stop laughing. He thought my adventure was the funniest thing he'd heard in a long time. Well, it wasn't funny to me at the time.

All I wanted was for him to pay my $25.00 fine and get me the hell out of Dodge. After a couple of hours, I was back in Belmont. I couldn't pack fast enough to return home where everything was familiar. I have to admit, it had been one hell of an eventful year. The cab I had called was waiting to take me to the airport where my flight was on time and ready to take me back to The ATL. See you in the spring when baseball season starts over again.

Spring Training 1962

It was early fall of 1961 when I decided to get married. I don't remember the date but it was sometime in September that I married a girlfriend from high school. I didn't do much the rest of the year because I was getting adjusted to married life. My buddies, Eugene Anderson, Mack Jones and I did a little club hopping for our boys' night out.

That's how I met Hank Aaron's brother, Tommie Aaron, who joined us from time to time that winter. I worked out a little whenever the weather would allow. In those days, the winter didn't cooperate much like today's weather does. I was simply marking time waiting for spring.

It didn't seem long before spring rolled around again and it was time to return to Arizona for spring training again. I left home in March, 1962 leaving a wife behind this time. I arrived back in Arizona excited to be there. Nothing had changed so it was easy to fall back into the routine. I met some new players this time; Frank Johnson, Ollie Brown, Dave Carter and a few others. This other player, Bob Perry, loved Etta James music. He played her album after practice until bed time every night. That has to be the reason why I love Etta James today. If I close my eyes, I can still hear her singing "At Last," "I Want A Sunday Kind of Love," or "Trust in Me." Things were going well for me in practice every day. After about a week into spring training, I was feeling good about myself. My batting average was over three hundred and I was playing well in the field. Life was good.

One morning, on my way into the dining room for breakfast, I saw my name on the notice board. It said report to the office at 9:30 am. Everybody knew what that meant. I would be released that day. I reported to the office and was given my pink slip. There was no meeting to explain; no reasons were given; nothing. I was shocked because this came out of the blue without any warning. I didn't understand. From my perspective,

I had been doing well and progressing every day. This wounded me deeply. I never really recovered from this decision. Several players expressed to me their confusion concerning how I got cut and they didn't. They knew I was the better player. As I was heading back to my room to pack I observed Buddy Kerr, my Quincy, Illinois manager, coming in my direction. I swear, when he saw me, he changed direction and went the opposite way from me. My first thought was that he could not face me. He wanted to avoid me. That convinced me. He was the one responsible for giving me the ax, thereby ending my career in professional baseball. I don't know for certain that he was the cause but that doesn't stop me from thinking it.

Everything was a blur. I quickly packed my bags, said my goodbyes and left for the airport. The flight back to Atlanta was rough. My mind was racing. I had so many unanswered questions going around and around in my head. When I arrived back home so soon, everyone was asking questions and making up their own mind about what happened. They didn't understand it either.

CHAPTER 2

BITTERNESSS

A Dream Denied

Loss of a Dream

I didn't talk about my release from the Giants to many people because it hurt too much. I didn't play baseball that summer because I was grieving for the loss of my dream. The pain, the hurt, the disappointment, the dishonesty, the frustration and the mystery of my being released caused me to become a very bitter man for a while. I lost interest in everything including baseball.

Later that year, I hear about the tryout camp for baseball at Ponce de Leon Park, in Northeast Atlanta. After much soul searching, I decided to go. I went with three or four of my buddies including Leroy Bowden to the park. Upon our arrival, we were informed that we could not try out at Ponce de Leon Park.

No reason was given for our rejection to participate. When we thought about it, we realized integration was still new in Atlanta and hadn't reached the parks, yet. It was relayed to us that tryouts for Black hopefuls were being held at four o'clock at Mosley Park, the park for Blacks.

I don't know why we thought five black men would be admitted to a Whites' only park. I have to laugh as I think about this. However, what really pissed me off, at the time, was there hadn't been any notice stating anything about two tryouts; one for Whites and one for Blacks.

We had had to be there by eight o'clock that morning. Now they were telling us we had to wait until 4:00 for tryouts for Blacks at Mosley Park. The distance wasn't a problem since the two parks weren't that far apart. Ponce de Leon Park was in Northeast Atlanta and Mosley Park was in Northwest Atlanta. Needless to say, I went since I'm not a quitter. Once I start something, I finish it.

These coaches informed us in so many words that we couldn't play; we weren't good enough. That was it for me for that entire year. I hated baseball at that moment and everything associated with it. That included all the people connected to baseball, too.

Not only had I been blindsided and sidelined from the love of my life, my old neighborhood, Rockdale, had been torn down. The neighborhood was gone and so was the ballpark where I had spent my entire youth. There was no more baseball there. I had nothing to do with baseball the remainder of that year. This was the end of the road for me. It was 1962. I was only twenty years old. I felt like a bruised, battered and weary old soldier.

Analyzing My Career With the Giants

It was several years before I was able to analyze the sequence of events that led to the end of my career with the Giants. When I signed the contract, I was 18 years old, a recent high school graduate with a small frame and weighing about 165 pounds. My upper body was very strong and I had tremendous speed. I could run the forty-yard dash in 6.03 seconds and I was timed running to first base in 3.03 or 3.04 seconds. I was a long ball hitter when the Giants signed me. However, when I got to training camp, everyone wanted me to try to hit the ball on the ground and use my speed.

The organization had a theory that players with a small build like mine should hit the ground ball and use their speed to get to first base. In the case of larger players, they wanted them to become the powerhouse home run and long ball hitters to bring all runners home to safety. That was not a bad idea but what they were asking was unnatural for me.

They wanted to strip away everything they had seen me do in Atlanta and make me over into some vision they had for the position I had been hired to fill. That's what they wanted so, that's what I tried to do. Let me tell you, it wasn't pretty. It was like asking me to stop writing with my right hand and start using my left. You can imagine what that would look like.

In my case, my whole game changed. My attempts to change weren't too successful. As I reminisce about my time with the Giants, I now understand how my inability to adapt to their method of playing was probably one of the things that held me back.

Racial prejudice, baseball's nemesis at that time, was always suspected when relating to Black players. Whatever the reason, baseball, after all, is a business. I understood that. During my era, it was not to the coach's advantage to trust a player's innate talent, ability or skill. It was all about the unwritten formula for winning; small players hit balls to the ground and larger players hit the long ball for the power play.

I learned a lesson from that experience. I taught my son and a lot of kids I coached to be respectful, no matter what. They were not to talk back or dispute any directions or corrections from their coach. They were instructed to just say "yes sir" or "no sir" then go out on the field and do what their body felt best doing and suffer the consequences later.

I honestly believe I could have played professional baseball for a much longer period if I had been permitted to use my body in the manner that was best for me. The reason(s) for letting me go will forever remain an unanswered question in my mind.

1963 – A Second Chance

For the remainder of 1962, I sat around, not doing very much. I was through with baseball. I was very bitter. Things also got a little uneasy around the home front. As the days and months rolled by, my money began to run out. As you know, when money goes out the front door, love goes out the back. Another dream crumbled.

During the winter of 1962, my longtime friend, Eugene Anderson, was away playing basketball with the Harlem Magicians Basketball team. I had no idea he was no longer playing baseball. Life is strange like that. He met Satchel Paige while on the road and learned that Satchel would be forming a team in the spring. Eugene immediately called me to ask if I would be interested in playing in the 1963 season. Remember, I was through with baseball.

I no longer liked the sport, that is, until the mention of the name, Satchel Paige. All those thoughts flew right out the window. I told him he didn't have to ask me twice. He, in turn, contacted Satch and asked him to offer me a contract. I didn't know how Eugene was going to work this so I didn't get my hopes up too high. After all, this was Satchel Paige, the greatest pitcher ever in the Negro League. The offer arrived and I accepted. Now, it was just a matter of waiting and staying in shape until spring. I did just that. This was meant to be a new beginning for me. I was set for 1963.

CHAPTER 3

A NEW BEGINNING
"Satchel Paige All-Stars"

PRE-SEASON; RALEIGH, NORTH CAROLINA

The Satchel Paige All-Stars

There's something special about spring. You can smell it in the air. You can see it everywhere you look. The earth seems to be changing and making preparations for America's favorite pastime, BASEBALL. Raleigh,

North Carolina here I come. My adrenaline is pumping. I've become revitalized. I'm on my way to meet Satchel Paige and play for his team, The Satchel Paige All-Stars. Eugene Anderson, my friend since high school, was already on the All Stars' roster.

During the winter months while we were at home, Eugene was instrumental in getting Satch to sign me as well as another former player, Leroy Bowden, from the Archer High School baseball team. Satch trusted Eugene's insight as well as his input for the betterment of the team. Now there were three of us; Eugene, Leroy and me, Ronald Smith. We made plans to travel from Atlanta together on our way to training camp in Raleigh, North Carolina. We arrived sometime in March and began practicing. Satch had not arrived yet.

Satchel Paige

The owner of the team was Arthur Dove, a little old rich black man, who had made his fortune from several enterprises such as renting pool tables and owning a successful and thriving juke box business. Most of the games we were to play were going to be fundraisers for a lot of small American cities. Satchel Paige had been set up as a drawing card because people would flock to the games just to see him play. Satch had a sweet contract.

He would be paid about $2,000 a game and he had to pitch only two innings per game. He was the star. His salary was much higher than all other players. This didn't matter to us because we could tell it was going to be a fun season. We were going to be playing baseball with the famous Satchel Paige. I don't know about the other players but that was more than enough payment for me. After about two weeks in North Carolina, Satch showed up and we were all introduced.

Yes, I had heard about Satch, the best and fastest pitcher in the Negro League and Major League and now I was meeting him in person. I saw this tall man, about 180-190 pounds, around 6'3"; walk into the room where we were gathered. He wasn't a muscular man, just solid. I noticed his long arms and big hands and he was carrying a briefcase. He looked like a business man, not a baseball player. For a big man, he spoke in a mild tone. Although he was not a good-looking man, people were drawn to his larger than life personality. You couldn't be out of sorts if you were in his presence since he was so much fun to be around.

Satch was a natural born comedian. He was a funny, funny man. Plus, he was an outstanding story teller. Sometimes he reminded me of a grandfatherly figure because of his demeanor. Whenever he left a place, it was as though a light had gone out and it was difficult to rekindle the bright spirit that Satch took with him. He also took something else, that briefcase. That intrigued me to the point of making up stories about what was in it. He was rarely seen without the mysterious briefcase. I vowed to ask him one day; after I got up enough nerve to do so.

Making History

At that time, it never occurred to me that I was making history, too, by playing on this world-famous icon's team. Here I was, Ronald MacArthur Smith, on the same team with one of the greatest baseball players in the world. I must admit I felt humbled and honored that he even considered me to be good enough to play on his team. I owe a debt of gratitude to Eugene Anderson for recommending me to the great Satchel Paige.

In order for the team to hit the road, we had to have transportation. The owner Arthur Dove solved that problem. He went to a Ford dealer and purchased a brand- new van that seated seventeen people. Imagine my shock, first and surprise, later when he walked up to me and said,

"Son, you are the driver."

I don't know why I was chosen but I guess in three weeks he had observed my responsible and competent nature and leadership ability. He never said and I never asked. I simply took the keys and started driving the bus.

The first few games were considered preseason games. After one of these games, Leroy was at the wheel driving us back to Raleigh. Everyone was asleep and Satchel Paige was riding with us this time. He always rode the team bus when his wife didn't come to the game. If she came, quite naturally he would ride back with her. Anyway, it was late and very dark where we were. Leroy accidently ran off the road onto the soft shoulder. The sudden bump shook the van and everybody in it, waking us out of a sound sleep. Nobody was happy with Leroy especially Satch. In fact, he asked Leroy Bowden,

"Son, what is your problem?"

Leroy replied, "Nothing." Satch then asked Leroy, "What did you say your name was?"

Leroy replied, "My name is Leroy." Satch then said, "Well then, I need to change my name from Leroy."

For those of you who don't know, his real name is Leroy "Satchel" Paige. I asked,

"What will you change your name to Satchel?" He replied,

"Oh hell, I don't know; maybe Grit Paige or Sausage Paige. I got to make sure it's anything but Leroy."

I guess you can tell from his response what he liked to eat. Everybody in the van just fell out laughing, including Leroy, the driver. Unfortunately for Leroy, his hitting skills, during the practice games, weren't up to par. He was released from the All Stars not too long after the bus incident. I really hated to see him leave. We had been friends since elementary school.

NEW SEASON: CHICAGO, ILLINOIS

Ron On the Bench

In April, we left North Carolina and headed to Chicago to start our season. The team was based in a hotel near Sixty-second and Cottage Grove. This hotel was owned by a black man. It was as nice as the white hotels I had stayed in previously. At the start of the season, we played about two weeks in cities around Chicago.

I was off my game. I didn't hit for about two weeks and I was benched. I had to deal with the situation even though I wasn't too pleased about it. I wasn't pleased with my performance either.

Thank God for Willie Washington, one of the coaches. He supported me and stayed in my corner. I appreciated him for that. It helped keep my spirits up. He kept advocating for me to play and stressing the point that I could hit. He didn't let up because he never lost faith in my ability to play and play well. One Sunday while in Ohio, we had a larger crowd than usual. Satchel asked me to warm him up as he was preparing to go into the game. There was no bull pen to warm up pitchers since this was a makeshift baseball park. Satchel and I went down the left field line. I put a glove down on the ground for him to throw over. He loudly hollered,

"What's that?" I hollered back, "It's your target." He yelled,

"Nooooooooo!"

He walked over to me, reached into his hip pocket and pulled out a piece of chewing gum wrapper. He asked me to put it down which I did. He then asked that I pick it up so he could see where I put it. I complied with his request. I took that gum wrapper and lifted it up high then put it back down in the grass. He proceeded to throw the ball right over that wrapper every time. This wasn't happening. How could he see the wrapper in the grass? I couldn't believe what I was seeing. However, he did it time after time after freaking time and I'm a witness. This man's pitching skill is unbelievably awesome!

That night, later in the game, we were trailing the other team by a couple of runs. Larry LAGrande, the manager, expressed a need for a pinch hitter. Everyone kind of looked in my direction and dropped their head. Satch said openly,

"No, not Lefty."

After noticing the not so subtle nod in my direction by team members. Willie Washington, one of the coaches, spoke up entreatingly,

"Hey Larry, let Lefty hit." In my mind I was chanting,

"Yeah, Larry, let Lefty hit. Let Lefty hit. Yeah, let Lefty hit."

I was known back then as Lefty since I played baseball as a left handed player although I am right handed. Larry finally gave in, against his better judgment, and told me to get a bat. I hurriedly got off the bench. I didn't want him to have time to change his mind. I was pumped up by his decision to give me a chance to do something that would help the team. I approached the plate with a determination not to blow this chance to prove to the team, coaches and management that I belonged here on this team. It was time to take action and produce. I placed my feet firmly on the ground, got into my stance then raised my bat in anticipation of the pitch. I never took my eyes off the pitcher. He got into his pitching motion and threw the ball. I made good contact because I hit a grand slam homerun on the first pitch. The team was overjoyed. They were pounding each other, pointing and yelling. I wasn't able to hear what they were saying. I was too busy taking my run around the bases. I was ecstatic. The coaches and manager had finally observed my power behind the bat. After my performance that day, I didn't think they were going to continue to bench me.

Ron Off the Bench

That Sunday we played a double header and predictably I was called from the bench to start in the second game. Just like before, I hit another homerun. After that day, my confidence returned since it had taken a beating while sentenced to that bench while my teammates were enjoying what I most wanted to do, play ball. That Sunday, I left the game satisfied and elated that I had proved I was not a onetime homerun hitter. My team mates now knew they could relax when it was my turn at bat. We won both games. Willie Washington proudly exclaimed in a friendly tone of voice to the team and to the manager,

"I told you Lefty could hit." Celebrating Double Header Victory

After the two games, it was time to relax and celebrate our triumph. We discovered this night club not too far from where we were. Satch was in rare form that night just being his comedic self. Three of us, Satch included, were sitting at a table talking and joking around. It wasn't long before Satch spotted three women sitting alone at another table. He pierced me with a stare before telling me to go over there to their table and get those girls to come and join us. I whispered to Satch in a low voice,

"But I don't know those women."

What he was asking me to do was outside my comfort zone. He knew nothing of my shyness. How was I to explain without losing his respect? I needn't have worried. He replied,

"Hell, I didn't know you until I met you. So, go 'head on over there boy."

So, I got up unhurriedly, stood there for a moment before moving in the direction of their table. Somehow, I talked them into joining us. After we helped to seat them, Satch didn't waste a second getting acquainted with the young ladies. He focused in on one of the girls by asking her name. She replied Jeanette. Satch wanted to know more,

"Jeanette what?" he inquired.

"Christmas, my name is Jeanette Christmas." She tentatively replied.

"Well then baby, meet Santa Claus." He immediately exclaimed, without hesitation.

I just rolled my eyes and laughed but not too loudly. I couldn't understand how he could come up with something like that so fast and he didn't even crack a smile. This guy was admirable. He was smooth. He was one cool dude.

The next night after the ballgame, as we were leaving the park, a lady approached Satch about getting and autograph. She wanted to know if she would be able to get his autograph right then. Her explanation for not waiting in line was she had to leave because she was visiting from out of town. Satch, recognizing a line crasher at her best, replied to the lady,

"I am so sorry but you will have to wait in line because I'm from out of town, too."

He held his head high and walked purposefully away with that long striding walk of his.

SATCHEL PAIGE THE GRIOT

After playing several games in and around the Chicago area, it was time to pull up stake and move on to the next assignment, Beloit, Wisconsin. We settled in a hotel and played in this area for about a month. I can't recall the name of the city where we were scheduled to play; however, what happened next is a true story. Word got to us that the owner of a large business wanted to challenge Satchel Paige when the team arrived in town to play.

This well-known business owner wanted to bat against Satchel's pitching. He even went so far as to make an offer that couldn't be refused. He would give $10,000 dollars to the city's favorite charity if he wasn't successful at getting a base hit. However, if he did hit a ball thrown by Paige, he would have bragging rights. This wasn't our first time encountering someone wanting to determine if the hype about Satch was true. You have to realize people doubted what the Press had to say about his ability. You know the old adage, "Seeing is Believing."

When we arrived in town, we could see evidence of this upcoming exhibition. The city had pulled out all the stops promoting and advertising this event. The people of this small town were hyped. All the advertising had drawn a huge crowd to the game. The way this event was shaping up, reminded me of the old western movie, "Showdown at the OK Corral." The game was going along smoothly until the seventh inning when the atmosphere became charged with electricity. Satchel Paige took his place on the pitcher's mound. Remember now, he only pitched two innings per game.

You could feel the excitement and expectation emanating from the stands. The team was pumped up for Satch. We knew how good he was. We were waiting in anticipation of how Satch was going to strike this guy out. We knew ole Satch was going to give the people a show while, at the same time, earning $10,000 for the city's favorite charity.

Satch had warmed up and was waiting for his challenger to come to the plate. His demeanor screamed confidence; head held high, eyes focused on the target, body loose and relaxed, hands calm and steady, feet planted, ready for action. This guy was first at bat. It was evident he was no slouch. He put up a big fight fouling off pitch after pitch. Well ole Satch finally got tired of him. He looked over his shoulder at the infielders and told all of them to; sit down, take a load off, rest yourself. Next, he assuredly declared,

"Don't worry, because I got him."

The infielders followed his directive and sat down on the field. Can you imagine what was going through everybody's mind? They stared in amazement at the infielders out there sitting down as though they didn't have a care in the world. Everybody in attendance was about to find out. If you blinked, you missed what happened next. At the next pitch, the batter struck out. It was over just that fast. A roar went up from the crowd as they went wild in disbelief. The team joined in, too. That Satchel Paige sure could throw that ball.

After the game, a fan came up to Satch and did what many people did in those days and that was to question Satch about his age. This never failed to irritate him. The man asked Satch,

"How old are you? My father is sixty-five and his hair is grey." Satchel smiled as he replied,

"You want to see my hair?"

and quickly removed his cap to reveal a head of mixed gray hair without too much gray.

He continued,

"You want to know how I feel about age? Age is like mind over matter; if you don't mind, it don't matter."

We left the park and did our usual; going into town looking for a watering hole. That night, for some reason, we didn't linger. Instead the group returned to the hotel. No one was ready to turn in and call it a night. We were simply sitting around talking when Satch started talking about the old days. We enjoyed listening to Satch tell stories about his earlier experiences. He spoke fondly of a former roommate as well as teammate when they played for the Kansas City Monarchs. He was known only as "Cool Papa Bell".

I had heard this story before and I'm certain the others had heard it, too. You see, "Cool Papa Bell" was a baseball legend. If you played baseball, you had heard of Cool Papa Bell. However, it was different this time because we were in the presence of another legend, Satchel Paige himself recounting the story. It was amazing to hear this story coming from Satchel's own mouth. When asked if "Cool Papa Bell" was as fast as people said. Satch leaned back, looked at us and explained,

"Cool Papa Bell" was so fast that he could turn out the light and get into bed before the room got dark."

Now that's fast. What a way to describe a ball player. Satch was on a roll. He recounted another story about another pitcher on a former team he had played for. Satchel and his team arrived in town for a scheduled game. The other team's representative presented

Satchel's team with an unusual request. They inquired if Satch could sit out and not pitch in order to allow their team a chance at winning. They felt it was a done deal they would lose since they didn't have any illusion about being able to win with Satch pitching.

The team's manager thought it over and decided to let Satch sit this one out. I can't imagine this happening in today's NBL. Anyway, the other team's representative was even given the opportunity to select anybody they would like to see pitch against them. In my mind, I was thinking how different baseball had been back in the day. Satch continued the story. There was a little skinny guy sitting on the bench with no shoes on and they chose him. To their astonishment and regret, that little skinny guy without any shoes pitched a shutout against them. They had no idea that this guy was as good as Satchel Paige. He was known as "Shoeless Joe Johnson" not to be confused with the infamous, "Shoeless Joe Jackson" associated with the Black Sox scandal of that era. That Satchel Paige knew how to tell a story. Since Satch was in a jovial mood, I decided to ask him about the briefcase he carried with him all the time. I was thinking along the line of money or booze. When I mentioned to him what I had been thinking, he folded up into fits of laughter. He laughed so long and hard, I thought he was going to lose his breath.

He pointed to the case and told me to open it. It certainly wasn't money or booze, that's for sure. It was filled with nothing but home remedies such as; SSS, Witch Hazel, Cod Little Liver Pills, horse's liniment, rubbing alcohol, Castor Oil, Hadicol, aspirin, etc. He was walking around with his own little medicine cabinet. After making this discovery, I doubled over in laughter, too. I couldn't help myself.

SEASON'S END: Muscatine, Iowa

We played several games in the Muscatine area. Our stay there was uneventful. The people we met were interesting to interact with and they appeared interested in us. We weren't accustomed to being in a town without seeing other people of color. It was a little strange and uncomfortable at first but we got used to it the short time we were there.

Time was winding down as we prepared to play our last game in Muscatine. Afterwards, we returned to the hotel in a jovial mood to pack and made provisions to leave town. The next morning the team checked out of the Hotel. I checked out right along with them. They were moving on to the last stop of the season, Canada. However, I had an emergency back home and had made a decision not to travel with the team to Canada. Instead, I had made arrangements to go home for a few days and join them later. We said our goodbyes and farewells. Then they were gone.

I remained behind to catch a bus leaving Muscatine later that night. I had already planned what I was going to do until time to catch the bus. My plan was to return to my hotel room and kick back and enjoy this little leisure time relaxing, reading and listening to the radio. Little did I know what awaited me in this cozy little town without the team.

I turned around and ambled back into the hotel to check back in. This was the perfect arrangement. You will not believe what happened next. I approached the desk and asked the desk clerk if I could get a room. She explained, with all the frigidity of an Eskimo's nose, that they didn't have one available. I thought this to be mighty strange.

So, I proceeded to inquire if she could give me the room I had just vacated. Again, the answer was no. She briskly informed me that it had to be cleaned, first. I'm not getting it. I'm not realizing what's really going on. I encouragingly stated that I didn't mind about the room being cleaned since I had only checked out ten minutes ago. In my mind, I was thinking this was a no brainer. Give me a key and I will return upstairs with no problem. When she replied firmly,

"No sir, I can't do that. The room won't be ready until 3:00 pm."

Then it hit me. Without the team, I was just a black man trying to book a room in this hotel and that &¢@/%# didn't want me there. The team had already left and there I was, all alone. I controlled my anger enough to ask if I could leave my bags in the lobby. Surprisingly, at least to me, she gave me permission to do that. I left the hotel with the idea of locating a movie or something in order to kill a few hours until time for my bus. I was casually walking around town. I noticed a gas station and the gas attendants were all white men. Where I come from, those jobs were performed by black men. Next I observed a trash truck. All the workers on it were white, also. That was very, very strange to me. I had never in my entire life seen a white man on a trash truck. Black men were hired to work those menial jobs.

It took a while but it finally occurred to me that I was the only dark person in this lily-white town. Where in the hell was I? I continued on until I located the movie theater.

Ahhh! I can go in here, get off the street, where I am too visible, and relax. The movie didn't open until that evening. What kind of place was this? I knew right then I had to try to get the hell out of there. I was beginning to feel paranoid. I knew where the bus station was and went there. A Greyhound bus was arriving as I was approaching the station. When it parked, I ran up to the driver and blurted out,

"Sir, where is this bus headed and how long is your layover?"

He replied, "Saint Louis, Missouri is my next stop." Checking his watch he stated,

"Layover is about ten or fifteen minutes."

I wanted to know if he could wait until I got my bags from the hotel. He told me I would have to hurry. I ran to that hotel like I was sprinting to home base. My imagination was working overtime. I gathered my bags quickly because I sensed it was past time for me to get the hell out of Dodge.

I did exactly that. I bought me a ticket to Saint Louis, Missouri and got on that bus. It couldn't leave fast enough for me. The destination didn't matter nor the direction as long as I was leaving this town. That was a scary experience for me; being the only black in an all-white town.

Stories of black men disappearing and never being heard from again were spinning around in my head.

Memories of being arrested in North Carolina returned. Although nothing happened, a tiny voice whispered, it could have.

I finally realized that old brother racism had raised its head once again. I didn't think it existed in the Mid-West. As I aged and continued to travel, I realized segregation and racism can pop up anywhere. As I reminisce about my experience in Iowa, it makes me wonder if that little town has changed. I think I'll add Muscatine, Iowa to my list of places to visit in the future.

CHAPTER 4

TIME FOR A CHANGE
"The Atlanta Cardinals"

TIME FOR A CHANGE

Since I was no longer playing baseball, I had to find a job quick, fast and in a hurry. It didn't take long because I was a man on a mission. I didn't like being without funds. When I applied to The Carling Brewing Company, they hired me on the spot. It was the fall of 1963. I was 23 years old.

I met a guy by the name of Elmer Mixon. Both of us were social animals and we hit it off immediately. In fact, we became close friends. I am a firm believer that people come into your life for a reason and so it was with Elmer Mixon. It took a lot of concentration, stops and pauses not to call him Nixon. He and I were constantly discovering new things about each other. It wasn't long before the topic of baseball came up. That's when he revealed how involved he was in the sport of baseball.

In fact, he was a member of The Atlanta Cardinals, a semi-pro local team. Their schedule boasted about fifty to sixty games each summer and they played only on the weekends. Mixon tried his best to convince me to come and play with them during the next season but I refused. I must admit, I was tempted but only for a moment. I knew the manager, Frank Anthony, a man I had never liked. To be truthful, I totally disliked him. The man had never done anything to me. I just didn't like his vibes. One never knows how things are going to work. Once I got to know Frank Anthony, we ended up being great friends later on down the road.

Later that year, Mixon sent the owner of the Atlanta Cardinals to visit me at my house. This was almost déjà vu because it reminded me of the time when the manager of the San Francisco Giants visited me in my home in Atlanta. The owner, Sam Jones, introduced himself and revealed the reason for his visit. He wanted me to come and play on his team.

I wasn't really interested in playing for the Atlanta Cardinals and I was trying to create a reason that sounded believable. After all, it isn't every day that the owner of a sports team shows up at your front door to personally ask you to become a part of his team.

I explained that I didn't have baseball on my mind because I was worried about my bills. He asked how much were they? Since that wasn't the real reason, I blurted out the first number that came into my head, one hundred dollars. Without missing a beat, Sam Jones reached for his wallet, extracted a one hundred dollar bill and offered it to me. He ended our conversation when he turned to walk toward the door. When he got to the door and opened it, he looked at me over his shoulder and said, "See you at practice tomorrow."

I had not moved since he placed that one hundred dollar bill in my hand. That was totally unexpected. He caught me off guard. Now I was chiding myself for not having asked for more. A hundred dollars back in the day was a lot of money. By accepting Sam's money, I was now committed to showing up for practice. That is the true story of how I came to play on the Atlanta Cardinals' team.

Upon my arrival at the field, I was surprised to see a lot of players I had played against in high school. I already knew most of the team. We had a mini-reunion right there on the field. Frank Anthony, the manager, had done his homework. Only the best players from all of the Atlanta Black high schools had been solicited to form this team. That was a fun team. We were good and we knew it. The Atlanta Cardinals was the team to beat during those days. We won a lot of games during my twenty-five years playing with them. We traveled a lot especially in and around the southeastern states.

We played in places like Rickwood Field located in Birmingham, Alabama. This field is known as the oldest baseball stadium in America. We also traveled to Tallahassee, Florida, Memphis, Tennessee, Mississippi, Montgomery, Alabama and all over the state of Georgia. For a long time, if you can believe this, our home games were played at Ponce de Leon Ballpark, the same place that the Atlanta Crackers played. This information will have no meaning for you unless you were born and raised in the South. Black people could attend the games at Ponce de Leon Ballpark but had to sit in a reserved section without a good view. Although The Cardinals were allowed to play there, we could only use the park when The Atlanta Crackers were traveling.

After a few years of playing with the Atlanta Cardinals, I met Walter Dockery. Little did I know what an impact he would have on my career as well as my life. He had been watching me and decided I was who he wanted to umpire the Little League games. My vision had always involved playing baseball. Umpiring the game had never entered my mind. However, I thought what the hell. I'll give it a try. I immediately purchased a rule book and started studying it right away.

My other preparations included buying equipment that was both required and needed for this job. Before long I was working as an umpire earning about $8.00 dollars a game. Talking about on the job training, it was certainly challenging. I developed into a decent umpire after a few years. I enjoyed every moment out there on the field umpiring.

As my memory reaches back into the archives of events during this period of my life, I will never forget this particular event. One night after finishing up an early game, I agreed to go with some friends to a basketball game in Gainesville, Georgia. I was to park my car, leave it and ride with them. At the last minute, I backed out and decided not to go. They left and went on without me. Later that night, I got a call informing me there had been an accident. There were four people in the car I was supposed to have traveled in.

The driver and his two sons were killed instantly. One other passenger in the car, Andre Patillo, a teenager, survived the accident. That was a life changing moment not only in his life but also mine as well. I vowed to do whatever I could for this kid to keep him from falling through the cracks. I later coached him at Morehouse College an HBCU in Atlanta, Georgia.

That teenager has become a fine young man. In fact, he is the current athletic director at Morehouse College. I am still in contact with him today.

We Met Our Match

"Go sit down! Next!"

My playing days with the Atlanta Cardinals was a lot of fun. We had a great team and a very proud team. We didn't lose many games because we didn't like losing. We became the team to beat. Our reputation followed us wherever we played. Competition was the name of the game within our team since each player had been a star on his high school team. Placing all these egos together sometimes caused problems within the ranks. Our egos didn't permit us to error in the eyes of our team mates. This pushed us to play our best, at all times, so that one or maybe two of us would stand out and have bragging rights for that game.

On one of our trips to Florida, we met out match. This team was an improvement over the others we had been playing. In fact, they came prepared to play. They had a guy pitching for them that was very, very good and he knew it. He did something I had never seen before and I never saw again. The guy was pitching a good game but he was talking trash to all of our players that came to the plate. He would point to a Cardinal player and say something like,

"Okay, so, you're next."

He would proceed to strike out the hitter, afterwards saying, "Go sit down. Next!"

He did that throughout the entire game. I was not in the lineup to play that game so I had a front row seat to his antics. I was sitting on the bench burning up. We had had a double header that day and I had played in the first game. Now I was sitting out the second game which was my policy. I was getting older and couldn't play double headers like I used to. I would The game was tight and this other team was leading by one run. We reached the late innings and he walked a batter. Our manager, Frank Anthony, called me to pinch hit. Needless to say, I was eager to get up to the plate because I wanted to shut this guy up. As I started to the plate to pinch hit, the catcher looked at me, stood up and started out to the mound to have a word with the pitcher. The pitcher saw him coming and they met half way. I overheard the catcher inform the pitcher to be cautious with me because he thought I was a good hitter. The pitcher replied,

"Don't worry about him. I got him. If he could hit that well, he would be playing."

I stepped into the batter's box and he quickly threw two strikes right by me. I missed the first two pitches. Now I'm thinking this guy is as good as he thinks he is. I had to step out of the box and try to get it together. He then threw two balls outside and I took both of them. I was ready for the ball. The next pitch that he threw, I hit it over the center fielder's head and off the fence. I ended up on third base with a sliding triple. After I got up and dusted off, I yelled to the pitcher,

"I bet you'll listen to your catcher next time."

I was a happy man. We won the game. The funniest thing happened about a couple of weeks after that game. I wish I could remember that pitcher's name and the name of the team he played for. Anyway, I walked into practice and there he was. He was now playing for the Atlanta Cardinals. Frank Anthony always wanted the best players on his team. It was not uncommon for him to make a move like that. We thought we were good before. Now with the acquisition of this pitcher, we were great.

Playing to Impress

Thinking about that game in Florida made me remember an incident at another game. The Atlanta Cardinals were playing a team from Manchester,

Georgia. I was having a good day at the plate. I had brought a young lady to the game because she had expressed a desire to see me play. I was no different from any other man. I was trying to impress my lady. My first two times at the plate, I hit back to back home runs. I had done that a lot of times before so it was no big deal to me. After I hit the second home run, the manager of the other team screamed at the pitcher,

"What are you throwing?"

Everyone thought that was funny. The next inning, the manager of the Manchester team decided that he would take the mound and pitch. I guess he felt he could do a better job. I hit two more home runs off of him. The pitcher that he replaced, screamed out to the manager,

"What did you throw?

We beat them pretty bad. Oh yeah! I did impress my lady. She surprised me with a reward for my hard day's work.

Kirkwood Park: The Cardinals New Home

A lot of changes were taking place that concerned the general welfare of the team. First, Frank Anthony, the manager of the Cardinals, had taken over as the new owner of the team. He was now both owner and manager. The previous owner, Sam Jones, had gotten too old and was no longer interested in being the manager. In my opinion, he made the right decision.

Sam Jones had been the owner of the Cardinals since I was a little kid and just beginning to learn the game of baseball. As a teenager, I had the pleasure of playing against his team when he brought them to Rockdale for a game. They were called The Southern Cardinals at that time. I never imagined that one day I would be playing for his team, The Atlanta Cardinals.

Frank Anthony was a different story. He didn't play baseball, never had played and didn't know the first thing about managing a team of great players. We managed the team. We decided the strategy for each game. However, anything involving money was directed to Frank. We respected and admired Frank because he was a hustler, a hardworking man. He had three jobs. He threw papers for The Atlanta Daily World, a Black owned newspaper. He was employed by The Georgia Power Company. He also owned a cleaning company with contracts for several office buildings in downtown Atlanta. Like I said, Frank was a hardworking man. He used a lot of his own money to sponsor the team. Anything a player needed, Frank supplied it. But, he had a strange way of giving the players what they needed. If a request was made for a new glove, he would purchase it and put it in a place where you could see it. You had to take it because he wasn't going to give it to you. After you took the equipment, he would fuss about how you didn't take care of stuff, etc. He was an unusual man, but in a good way. Whenever we played out of town, payment was always on a sixty - forty basis with The Cardinals receiving the forty. The players didn't receive any of the earnings. We didn't even think about it because we understood where the money was going. Our team had the best equipment; the best gloves, bats, balls, uniforms, cleats, etc. Frank really cared about the team.

Next, we had grown weary of searching for a place to play when The Atlanta Crackers played at home. As a Black team, we were accustomed to playing just about anywhere. But, that was then and this was now. Times were changing and we needed to change in order to keep up with the times. We had to come to the realization that taking hand-me-downs and seconds from the White community was no longer acceptable. Just as we no longer were regulated to the back of the bus, we didn't need to play in a park where we knew we were only tolerated. It was time to relocate to a site where we could feel comfortable and our fans could relax, too. The Atlanta Cardinals eventually left Ponce de Leon Park as a home site. It was time for the Cardinals to have their own home site better suited for the team and our needs.

Kirkwood Park was an ideal site. It was located in a nice community. That was a major requirement for our home site. The park was great. The field was great. However, the amenities were horrible. It was comical, at best. First, there was no fence around the field. Correction, there was a fence in left field but that was the only part of the field that had fencing. There was a big tree in right field. I remember that tree well. I hit a lot of home runs over that big tree in right field. A street, with lots of houses, ran behind center field and right field. I wish I could draw a picture. The ground rule at Kirkwood Park was any ball hit into the street was a home run. I kid you not. That was the ground rule. It made me think about when I played baseball as a kid. In my neighborhood, and I have to make that distinction because rules changed from neighborhood to neighborhood. As I was saying, in my neighborhood, if you hit the ball over the building, that was an out. If you hit the ball over the two story house, that was an out. We concentrated on what constituted an out. If we couldn't make a play, that was considered an out.

I worked for a TV rental company that left me pretty much on my own since I was making deliveries all day. I remember one Saturday, we had a game and I couldn't take off. I couldn't let the team down so I did what anyone who loved baseball would have done. I drove the company van to the game and parked it on the street. I knew I wasn't supposed to be out at the park during working hours. But I couldn't miss my game. As luck would have it, I hit a ball into the street, a homerun, and broke the windshield of the van. That was my dilemma. I got into a little trouble with my supervisor but I was able to work it out. After all, I was a good worker and he appreciated my honesty.

Another time, on a Sunday, we were playing a game and I hit a home run over the street and it went into one of the houses. It was a two story house and the ball evidently went in the upstairs portion. A few minutes later, a lady came over to the ball field and went directly to the manager Frank Anthony. She came to return the ball. She also wanted to inform him that we had interrupted her while cooking dinner. She wasn't very pleased because the ball I had hit had landed in her pot of collard greens. She appeared not to be too mad because her son Gus was our bat boy. I believed she was making up the part about the ball landing in her pot. I'm not saying it didn't or couldn't have happened. After all, it provided material for a good baseball story.

McCoy Park: The Cardinals On The Move Again

After a few years, The Cardinals moved from Kirkwood Park to McCoy Park in Decatur Ga. We arrived early for the very first game to acclimate ourselves to our new surroundings. Plus, we needed the extra time to get ready to play. I guess the people in the neighborhood had received word that The Atlanta Cardinals were going to McCoy Park to play. A few fans were already there to greet us.

I remember this little old White man was sitting in the bleachers. I sat down to change my shoes not far from where he was sitting. After a few minutes, he leaned over and asked,

"Hey boy, can any of you boys hit that ball over that fence out there?"

I squinted my eyes and looked in the direction he was pointing. I didn't answer right away because I was trying to determine where he was going with this question. Eventually I turned around and looked up at him and responded,

"I don't know, maybe we can."

He revealed his purpose for asking when he said,

"Well, I've only seen one person hit that school building behind that fence. That person was Mike Ivey and now he plays for the San Diego Padres."

"Is that so?"

was my only response as I got up to rejoin the team. I didn't have any time for small talk at that moment. The game started soon after that. Sometime, later during the game, I hit a ball so long that it sailed high over the fence to the top of the school building hitting the air conditioning unit. The momentum of my ball was traveling with such speed and force that it left a dent in the AC unit. After the game, I noticed old pops was still there. I couldn't help myself. I had to say something. I walked over and I said to him, "Now you have seen two people hit that building: Mike Ivey from the San Diego Padres and Ron Smith from The Atlanta Cardinals."

I left McCoy Park a happy man that day.

CHAPTER 5

UMPIRING
A NEW GIG

Umpiring A New Gig

While umpiring, I had no interest in coaching at all. I tremendously enjoyed what I was doing. However, my son was playing baseball, at the time, and doing quite well. The coaches he had were good guys but, in my opinion, they sucked as coaches. I used to go to his practices and watch from the sidelines. That's how I discovered the coaches weren't teaching the team correctly.

I knew the game but I didn't want to coach. It hurt to watch my son's team screw up game after game. I would then go home and try to straighten out all the bad coaching at home with my son. I soon started attending his games on a regular basis. While there, I was that parent you see at every game who stands up and loudly criticizes the coach's decisions, the ump's calls.

One day a guy, sitting on the bleachers near me, suggested that since I seemed to know more than the coaches, I should go out there and help them instead of complaining and criticizing so much. Who was this guy? What right did he have to criticize me? I was mad as hell! Much later, after cooling down, I had time to think about his suggestion.

I realized what he had said made more sense than sitting in the bleachers giving those coaches hell. That's why, the next season, I started coaching my son. I was a man on a mission. If my son was going to play, he was going to learn to play correctly. I later learned that the guy who spoke to me at the game was Harvey Lottie, a coach himself. He was also the president of the Gresham Park Baseball Association which was in the area where he lived. This was a coincidence since I lived there, too.

Harvey Lottie had always been involved in community affairs. This didn't change when he and his family moved into the Gresham Park neighborhood. This was mostly an all-white community that the law of integration had touched. We now had the freedom to choose where we wanted to live, shop, work, eat, go to school, etc. This was not an easy time for anyone, Black or White. Harvey was new to the area. However, as he became more visible through his involvement, he was slowly accepted. Gresham Park belonged to the DeKalb Department of Recreation like all parks in the region. It had an outstanding reputation in the area of baseball due in part to its membership in the American Amateur Baseball Congress, a national organization.

This community had a unique association with the park. This community had come together to form the Gresham Park Civic and Athletic Association. It was this group of dedicated community servants who had devised a way to serve the entire neighborhood and its children. DeKalb County owned the land and facilities however The GPCAA was able to lease the park from the county during baseball and football season. The community paid for all upkeep, provided staff where needed, bought and paid for all equipment, uniforms and any other necessities. As I said, this was a unique organization. It boasted well over one thousand dues paying members.

The Black Gresham Park gained membership into the AABC by default. Harvey Lottie's children spent a lot of time at Gresham Park because they wanted to play baseball. With the influx of Black families and the exodus of White families, the neighborhood gradually changed.

The people who ran Gresham Park also left and went to another park, taking all the equipment with them. They must have moved it out under the cover of darkness. The next day when the children went to the park to play baseball, everything was gone; rakes, shovels, field line equipment, tractors, bases, bats, balls, and anything else you can think of. They couldn't take the scoreboard because that was stationary and owned by Coca Cola. We, the adult leaders, couldn't get too upset since we knew they had worked hard to finance every inch of their park. Now it was our park and we were going to have to do the same thing. We lived in a great neighborhood within walking distance of the well-known Gresham Park but we didn't have any baseball equipment.

After the shock wore off, the parents simply rolled up their sleeves in preparation for the work they were going to have to do to keep the park open and their children happy. The up side to inheriting the park meant that the neighborhood was now a member of the AABC by default. Our team(s) could play against other member teams in the all-white AABC. The door that was once closed was now wide open. The American Amateur Baseball Congress had to welcome its first Black team from Atlanta, Georgia. That was a fact that could not be denied and the Gresham Park team had to be added to the roster and included in scheduling, tournaments, etc. The Gresham Park's membership in the AABC was instrumental in paving the way for other Black teams in Atlanta to become members.

During the next six years, I continued to master the skill of umpiring. I acquired the umpire's book of rules and regulations for playing the sport of baseball. That book never left my body. I kept it in my pocket at all times. I studied that book from cover to cover as if my life depended on it. People began to notice me officiating at games and determined that I was not only good at my job, but I was also fair. Because of my reputation, I was selected to umpire for the regional baseball tournament three times. That was an accomplishment. In 1977, I was chosen to work a regional tournament run by the American Baseball Congress. This was an honor for me since this congress was made up of mostly white kids, coaches and officials.

And then I discovered I was chosen, not for my knowledge, skill and expertise, but as their token black umpire for that year. This shouldn't have surprised me but it caught me off guard. I had been thinking how much progress the American Baseball Congress had made and that baseball had come a long way in

Atlanta. The discovery that the more things change the more things remain the same saddened me. I was such an optimist at the time.

Each year, when tournament time rolled around, there was always a different excuse as to why I couldn't work some of the tournament games. The first excuse was, I was not an AABC member. So, I secretly obtained the needed information and joined the organization. I didn't tell anyone what I had done. The operative

word is "secret." If you don't want anyone to know your business, don't tell it. I was going to be ready for them next year with my membership in hand.

Tournament time arrived. and I was given the same story about not being a member. It was with great dignity and pride that I produced my membership card. I was informed with a smile that I was too late. All assignments had been distributed. It gave me great pleasure to out maneuver them, at first. You know how kids are; I'll show you. But I was no longer a kid. I was an adult looking for work in a field that I was qualified to do. It was time for action. If they thought they were going to get away with playing their little cat and mouse game, they had another thought coming.

I called my attorney, Henry Stringfellow, because I knew he had been around Dekalb County a long time and he was acquainted with many people in the field of law. He was a good lawyer and the fact that he was White increased my chances. I have no idea of what he did, what he said or who he talked to. The only thing I remember is things changed rapidly. My phone started ringing constantly and I began receiving offers from all over the county. I was now able to pick and choose assignments like everyone else. A strong determination and the will to go all the way along with my lawyer's actions had a tremendous impact on the future of Black umpires in Atlanta and the surrounding areas.

Two of my fellow umpires and I were given an assignment in a tournament in Hapeville, Georgia. A funny thing happened on the way to our new assignment. We were not in uniform when we drove up to the park to work the game. There was a little old White lady operating the gate and collecting money from those who had not previously purchased their ticket. She looked at us and said,

"That will be five dollars each sir."

I informed her we were there to umpire the game. That little old White lady couldn't contain her disbelief. She shrieked in an incredulous tone,

"You are here to do what?"

Then she got herself back together and politely told us where we could park. I wish I had a picture of that look she had on her face. Segregation is a beast but racism and stereotyping is larger. Integration destroyed the beast but had no effect on the other. Black and White teams had always been separated and they preferred it that way. They didn't want their kids on the same team with black kids.

Black Umpires Unite

The Capitol City Officials Association was established and still exists today because of some dissatisfied and concerned young umpires. It appeared that the younger members, this included me, were limited to umpiring at mostly B team and Little League games. We wanted to be able to officiate on all levels; B team, varsity, college, local and/or regional tournaments. The Quarterback Club was already established and organized but it was run by a clique of old high school coaches. They were the ones who decided who would officiate and where. We, the younger officials felt there was a need for an association for officials of all sports. We didn't want to be limited by the orders of The Quarterback Club. A group of officials decided to meet at Morris Brown College in Atlanta, Georgia for the purpose of forming such an association. The people present at this meeting were Frank Anthony, Walter Dockery, John Hanson, Bucky Speight, Robert Williams and I, Ronald Smith. Dockery and Hanson were already members of The Quarterback Club but they wanted to help younger officials get started. There were a few others whose names I've forgotten.

Due to the establishment of the Capitol City Officials Association, I worked for thirty years as a college and high school baseball umpire. I occasionally officiated at Little League and semi-professional league games. Over the years, I became very good at my craft and well respected in the field of umpiring.

Thirty Years "In" was the "End"

Umpiring was my agony and my ecstasy. I should have been the poster child for juvenile arthritis. By the time I began umpiring, the wear and tear on my knees, arms, wrists and back from playing and coaching were taking its toll. I was in constant pain. However, I was passionate about all aspects of this sport called baseball. Nothing could ever replace this feeling, this energy and this synergy. I lived and breathed baseball since the age of seven. Now, my body was beginning to betray me. When this started happening on a regular basis, I had to face reality and make a heartfelt decision. First, I admitted to myself that my knees were giving out and I was having difficulty bending and taking all the positions an umpire has to take. I had decided to give it thirty years. At the end of those thirty years, I would retire from umpiring permanently. I stayed true to my word. I remained on the job from 1964 - 1994. The season wasn't over on my anniversary date, but it was over for me.

I, like most umpires, carried my equipment and accessories around in the car so as to be ready at a moment's notice. The time had come to let it all go since I wouldn't be needing it anymore. I bought only the best gear and equipment plus, I had two of everything; chest protector, knee guards, arm protectors, etc. This was expensive stuff. While driving around trying to decide where to go first, I saw a young guy I knew from my coaching days approaching me from the other side of the street. We spoke hastily as he revealed he had passed the umpire test and was looking for gear and equipment. My mouth literally dropped open and my eyes became enlarged. I couldn't believe what I was hearing. I immediately told him to pull into the parking lot behind the bank. I stopped the car and motioned for him to get out and follow me. We arrived at the back of the car at the same time. He was totally in the dark.

He didn't know what was going on. I popped the trunk and gestured for him to look inside. This time, his mouth dropped open and his eyes almost bulged out of their sockets. He couldn't believe his good fortune. I have to give it to him. He was not greedy. He took one of everything he wanted. As he was looking over his bounty, it occurred to him how expensive umpire gear could be. He tentatively asked me how much for what he had. When I said fifty dollars, he nearly fainted. Both of us felt good about that unexpected transaction.

I completed my good deed of the day by distributing the remainder of the equipment among other umpires at various recreation centers. Thus, my thirty years umpiring for the state of Georgia came to an end. It was time to make another decision; orthoscopic scraping of the knees or knee replacement surgery. I chose knee replacement surgery and never looked back.

CHAPTER 6

COACHING

A Living Legacy

A PROTEST CALL

I didn't always enjoy umpiring and coaching at the same time. Working both areas of the game sometimes put me in unusual situations for example, one of the state championships during the seventies. It was so bizarre that I still remember what happened as if it were yesterday.

Late in the game, my team was losing. I was coaching third base. One of my players, Montrel Leonard, hit what I thought; my team thought, the other team thought and everyone watching the game thought was a go ahead home run. As he rounded the bases and approached third base, I pointed to the base to make sure he touched it. This was a habit of mine. I always did this to all my players. You would be surprised at the number of games that have been lost because someone forgot to touch the base. Anyway, Montrel touched the base and scored. The opposing coach informed the umpire that he missed touching third base. The umpire threw the pitcher the ball and he threw it to third base. The fielder caught the ball and touched the base and the ump hollered, "OUT." Well, knowing the rules as I did, I said, "BULL SHIT." I went to the ump and stated emphatically, "You can't appeal a play on a dead ball." Instead of addressing me, he went to the pitcher and told him the ball had to be put into play before he could appeal. So the pitcher took the ball again, went to the mound then stepped off. He then threw the ball to the third baseman who caught it and stepped on the base. This time, the ump yelled, "You're out." Shaking my head from side to side, I watched this mockery of the game playing out in front of me. They had no idea who they were playing with. I was extremely angry but determined to remain professional at all cost. I made my way determinedly toward the ump to protest the game at that point.

Before the tournament, coaches were given a sheet with rules and protest- charges and I had it in my back pocket. On that sheet, it stated clearly that in order to protest a game call, the fee was twenty-five dollars and it had to be paid in cash. However, the tournament director explained it would cost me one hundred dollars cash, if I wanted to protest. I said, "Okay, unhesitatingly. No problem, I'll pay it." They weren't expecting me to accept this blatant disregard for their own rules and charges. The game was put on hold until the protest decision was made.

On the way to the office to have my protest heard, the umpire and I had some words and he told me that I was out of the game. I laughed and told him he couldn't throw me out of the game because there was no game in progress. He turned beet red when I said that. I angered him further because I continued to respond in like manner to his angry tirade. Our verbal sparring was unceasing all the way to the meeting. I couldn't believe what I saw upon entering the office. I don't know what I was expecting but this certainly wasn't it. There sat an old white man chewing tobacco appearing to be about 80 years old. I thought I was seeing double when I looked around and saw another old man who appeared to be about the same age. Also in the room was a very large white woman. I knew her well. She was a tough cookie. She was going to recognize me just as I recognized her. It was all over for me. These three were the protest committee. I knew right then and there I didn't have a snowball's chance in hell of winning this protest. It was as it had always been; me against them or them against me. It didn't matter, I felt I was screwed and out of a hundred dollars anyway. The female member of the committee sometimes worked as a scoring official for the Gresham Park games. I'll never forget the time there was a question about a scoring discrepancy. The coach went to her and asked to see the score book. She refused him access, took the book and sat on it. That was a funny sight. Those of us who were there and witnessed this event still talk about it.

The ump presented his case first as part of the procedure. When my time came to speak, I just happened to have had a baseball rule book in my back pocket. Believe it or not, I don't know how in the hell I was able to turn to the page with the protest rule on it, but I did. That was better than standing there, turning pages, looking for it. I said what I had to say and read the rule to the committee. I then went back to the field to wait on their decision. We had been waiting for over a half hour when I saw the silhouette of the woman from the protest committee making her way slowly down the path toward our dugout. She was holding what looked like money in her hand. As she got closer, I could actually see the money in her hand. I was so relieved. This indicated that I had won the protest appeal. She approached me saying, "Coach, here's your money." Extending her hand, she returned my one hundred dollars. I was so happy with the results that I could have reached out and kissed that woman. Nahhhh, I wasn't that happy. We were able to finish the game without any more interruptions. That was a good day. Not only had this Black team won the protest appeal but we had also beat the White team fairly. Just another day in the Black man's world.

In The Safety Zone

The next day, I decided not to get into the coaching box to participate in the game. Coaching from the dugout would be my plan for this day of the tournament. I didn't want to present the umpires with any reason to come in contact with me. They were capable of using whatever they could to eject me from the game. These White umpires didn't like me because they couldn't control me. However, they respected me because of my proficient knowledge of the game.

Integration vs Segregation

All of these feelings of ill will derived from my past dealings with the umpires and the American Amateur Baseball Association. By denying work to some and limiting work to other umpires of color provided just cause for hiring a lawyer, which I did. This move didn't sit well with them. Since they were in charge of scheduling all the games, it was easy to continue that segregated mindset. This was during the time of the Civil Rights Movement and young Blacks were not afraid to go after and/or petition for what they wanted. The doors of opportunity had been knocked down and we were taking advantage of everything that was now available to us. We, the Black umpires, wanted to be afforded the same opportunities as the White umpires. Why couldn't we just get along? I also knew how they felt about me umpiring and coaching at the same time. In those days, not many people, or maybe no one but me, were doing both.

I was not able to turn a blind eye to what was happening on the field right in front of me. The umpire, on the bases, made a call that I didn't agree with. I knew I was going to regret stepping out of my self-imposed safety zone and going onto the field to protest the call. As I was expressing myself to the ump, one of the other umps came up to me and pushed me in my chest. His action infuriated me because I knew what he was trying to do. This was a tactic designed to provoke me enough so that I would react; then they could get me thrown out of the AABC. They hadn't counted on me not spontaneously reacting. I maintained my self-control. However, I looked the ump, who had pushed me in my chest, dead in the eye and declared angrily, "CRACKER," If you touch me again, I will kill you."

Call the Police

My threat resulted in being thrown out of the game as expected. I turned away immediately to walk away from the field. Before I could even get off the field, I heard sirens blasting from two police cars coming in the direction of the ball field. You would have thought someone had died or gotten robbed or something. The officers went immediately to the park officials who in turn pointed in my direction. They slowly approached the area where I was standing, hands on their weapon, ready. They wanted to know what was going on. My reply to them was that the umpire pushed me in my chest for protesting a call. I told him if he did it again, I would kill him. The policeman, in a firm tone, told me to calm down and stay away from the game. That was the end for that day. Believe it or not, the next day we were playing the park's home team. I watched in amazement as all the calls in the game went in our favor even thou the umpires were still angry because of the ruling on the protest the day before.

WE MET OUR MATCH

"Go sit down! Next!"

My playing days with the Atlanta Cardinals was a lot of fun. We had a great team and a very proud team. We didn't lose many games because we didn't like losing. We became the team to beat. Our reputation followed us wherever we played. Competition was the name of the game within our team since each player had been a star on his high school team. Placing all these egos together sometimes caused problems within the ranks. Our egos didn't permit us to error in the eyes of our team mates. This pushed us to play our best, at all times, so that one or maybe two of us would stand out and have bragging rights for that game.

On one of our trips to Florida, we met out match. This team was an improvement over the others we had been playing. In fact, they came prepared to play. They had a guy pitching for them that was very, very good and he knew it. He did something I had never seen before and I never saw again. The guy was pitching a good game but he was talking trash to all of our players that came to the plate. He would point to a Cardinal player and say something like,

"Okay, so, you're next."

He would proceed to strike out the hitter, afterwards saying, "Go sit down. Next!"

He did that throughout the entire game. I was not in the lineup to play that game so I had a front row seat to his antics. I was sitting on the bench burning up. We had had a double header that day and I had played in the first game. Now I was sitting out the second game which was my policy. I was getting older and couldn't play double headers like I used to.

The game was tight and this other team was leading by one run. We reached the late innings and he walked a batter. Our manager, Frank Anthony, called me to pinch hit. Needless to say, I was eager to get up to the plate because I wanted to shut this guy up. As I started to the plate to pinch hit, the catcher looked at me, stood up and started out to the mound to have a word with the pitcher. The pitcher saw him coming and they met half way. I overheard the catcher inform the pitcher to be cautious with me because he thought I was a good hitter. The pitcher replied,

"Don't worry about him. I got him. If he could hit that well, he would be playing."

I stepped into the batter's box and he quickly threw two strikes right by me. I missed the first two pitches.

Now I'm thinking this guy is as good as he thinks he is. I had to step out of the box and try to get it together. He then threw two balls outside and I took both of them. I was ready for the ball. The next pitch that he threw, I hit it over the center fielder's head and off the fence. I ended up on third base with a sliding triple. After I got up and dusted off, I yelled to the pitcher,

"I bet you'll listen to your catcher next time."

I was a happy man. We won the game. The funniest thing happened about a couple of weeks after that game. I wish I could remember that pitcher's name and the name of the team he played for. Anyway, I walked into practice and there he was. He was now playing for the Atlanta Cardinals. Frank Anthony always wanted the best players on his team. It was not uncommon for him to make a move like that. We thought we were good before. Now with the acquisition of this pitcher, we were great.

PLAYING TO IMPRESS

Thinking about that game in Florida made me remember an incident at another game. The Atlanta Cardinals were playing a team from Manchester, Georgia. I was having a good day at the plate. I had brought a young lady to the game because she had expressed a desire to see me play. I was no different from any other man. I was trying to impress my lady. My first two times at the plate, I hit back to back home runs. I had done that a lot of times before so it was no big deal to me. After I hit the second home run, the manager of the other team screamed at the pitcher,

"What are you throwing?"

Everyone thought that was funny. The next inning, the manager of the Manchester team decided that he would take the mound and pitch. I guess he felt he could do a better job. I hit two more home runs off of him. The pitcher that he replaced, screamed out to the manager,

"What did you throw?

We beat them pretty bad. Oh yeah! I did impress my lady. She surprised me with a reward for my hard day's work.

KIRKWOOD PARK

A lot of changes were taking place that concerned the general welfare of the team. First, Frank Anthony, the manager of the Cardinals, had taken over as the new owner of the team. He was now both owner and manager. The previous owner, Sam Jones, had gotten too old and was no longer interested in being the manager. In my opinion, he made the right decision. Sam Jones had been the owner of the Cardinals since I was a little kid and just beginning to learn the game of baseball. As a teenager, I had the pleasure of playing against his team when he brought them to Rockdale for a game. They were called The Southern Cardinals at that time. I never imagined that one day I would be playing for his team, The Atlanta Cardinals. Frank Anthony was a different story. He didn't play baseball, never had played and didn't know the first thing about managing a team of great players. We managed the team. We decided the strategy for each game. However, anything involving money was directed to Frank. We respected and admired Frank because he was a hustler, a hardworking man. He had three jobs. He threw papers for The Atlanta Daily World, a Black owned newspaper. He was employed by The Georgia Power Company. He also owned a cleaning company with contracts for several office buildings in downtown Atlanta. Like I said, Frank was a hardworking man. He used a lot of his own money to sponsor the team. Anything a player needed, Frank supplied it. But, he had a strange way of giving the players what they needed. If a request was made for a new glove, he would purchase it and put it in a place where you could see it. You had to take it because he wasn't going to give it to you. After you took the equipment, he would fuss about how you didn't take care of stuff, etc. He was an unusual man, but in a good way. Whenever we played out of town, payment was always on a sixty - forty basis with The Cardinals receiving the forty. The players didn't receive any of the earnings. We didn't even think about it because we understood where the money was going. Our team had the best equipment; the best gloves, bats, balls, uniforms, cleats, etc. Frank really cared about the team.

Next, we had grown weary of searching for a place to play when The Atlanta Crackers played at home. As a Black team, we were accustomed to playing just about anywhere. But, that was then and this was now. Times were changing and we needed to change in order to keep up with the times. We had to come to the realization that taking hand-me-downs and seconds from the White community was no longer acceptable. Just as we no longer were regulated to the back of the bus, we didn't need to play in a park where we knew we were only tolerated. It was time to relocate to a site where we could feel comfortable and our fans could relax, too. The Atlanta Cardinals eventually left Ponce de Leon Park as a home site. It was time for the Cardinals to have their own home site better suited for the team and our needs.

Kirkwood Park was an ideal site. It was located in a nice community. That was a major requirement for our home site. The park was great. The field was great. However, the amenities were horrible. It was comical, at best. First, there was no fence around the field. Correction, there was a fence in left field but that was the only part of the field that had fencing. There was a big tree in right field. I remember that tree well. I hit a lot of home runs over that big tree in right field. A street, with lots of houses, ran behind center field and right field. I wish I could draw a picture. The ground rule at Kirkwood Park was any ball hit into the street was a home run. I kid you not. That was the ground rule. It made me think about when I played baseball as a kid. In my neighborhood, and I have to make that distinction because rules changed from neighborhood to neighborhood. As I was saying, in my neighborhood, if you hit the ball over the building, that was an out. If you hit the ball over the two-story house, that was an out. We concentrated on what constituted an out. If we couldn't make a play, that was considered an out.

I worked for a TV rental company that left me pretty much on my own since I was making deliveries all day. I remember one Saturday, we had a game and I couldn't take off. I couldn't let the team down so I did what anyone who loved baseball would have done. I drove the company van to the game and parked it on the street. I knew I wasn't supposed to be out at the park during working hours. But I couldn't miss my game. As luck would have it, I hit a ball into the street, a homerun, and broke the windshield of the van. That was my dilemma. I got into a little trouble with my supervisor but I was able to work it out. After all, I was a good worker and he appreciated my honesty.

Another time, on a Sunday, we were playing a game and I hit a home run over the street and it went into one of the houses. It was a two-story house and the ball evidently went in the upstairs portion. A few minutes later, a lady came over to the ball field and went directly to the manager Frank Anthony. She came to return the ball. She also wanted to inform him that we had interrupted her while cooking dinner. She wasn't very pleased because the ball I had hit had landed in her pot of collard greens. She appeared not to be too mad because her son Gus was our bat boy. I believed she was making up the part about the ball landing in her pot. I'm not saying it didn't or couldn't have happened. After all, it provided material for a good baseball story.

KIRKWOOD PARK – THE CARDINALS NEW HOME

A lot of changes were taking place that concerned the general welfare of the team. First, Frank Anthony, the manager of the Cardinals, had taken over as the new owner of the team. He was now both owner and manager. The previous owner, Sam Jones, had gotten too old and was no longer interested in being the manager.

Next, we had grown weary of searching for a place to play when The Atlanta Crackers played at home. As a Black team, we were accustomed to playing just about anywhere. But, that was then and this was now. Times were changing and we needed to change in order to keep up with the times. We had to come to the realization that taking hand-me-downs and seconds from the White community was no longer acceptable. Just as we no longer were regulated to the back of the bus, we didn't need to play in a park where we knew we were only tolerated. It was time to relocate to a site where we could feel comfortable and our fans could relax, too. The Atlanta Cardinals eventually left Ponce de Leon Park as a home site. It was time for the Cardinals to have their own home site better suited for the team and our needs.

Kirkwood Park was an ideal site. It was located in a nice community. That was a major requirement for our home site. The park was great. The field was great. However, the amenities were horrible. It was comical, at best. First, there was no fence around the field. Correction, there was a fence in left field but that was the only part of the field that had fencing. There was a big tree in right field and a street ran behind center field and right field. I wish I could draw a picture. The ground rule at Kirkwood Park was any ball hit into the street was a home run. I kid you not. That was the ground rule. It made me think about when I played baseball as a kid.

There were a lot of houses along the other side of the street. I hit a lot of home runs over that big tree in right field. I remember once when I was working, I was pretty much on my own since I was making deliveries all day. We had a game that day and I couldn't take off. I couldn't let the team play so I did what anyone else would have done. I parked a company van that I was driving that day and wasn't supposed to be out at the park during working hours. As luck would have it I hit a ball into the street and broke the windshield of the van. I got into a little trouble with my supervisor but I was a good worker and I worked it out. One Sunday we were playing a game and I hit a home run over the street and it went into the house. The house was a two-story house and the ball evidently went upstairs because a few later a lady came over to the ball field and told the manager Frank Anthony that we interrupted her cooking dinner because the ball went into her collard green pot. She didn't get too mad because her son Gus was our bat boy.

McCoy PARK – DECATUR, GEORGIA

After a few years, The Cardinals moved from Kirkwood Park to McCoy Park in Decatur Ga. We arrived early for the very first game to acclimate ourselves to our new surroundings. Plus, we needed the extra time to get ready to play. I guess the people in the neighborhood had received word that The Atlanta Cardinals were going to McCoy Park to play. A few fans were already there to greet us.

I remember this little old White man was sitting in the bleachers. I sat down to change my shoes not far from where he was sitting. After a few minutes, he leaned over and asked,

"Hey boy, can any of you boys hit that ball over that fence out there?"

I squinted my eyes and looked in the direction he was pointing. I didn't answer right away because I was trying to determine where he was going with this question. Eventually I turned around and looked up at him and responded,

"I don't know, maybe we can."

He revealed his purpose for asking when he said,

"Well, I've only seen one person hit that school building behind that fence.

That person was Mike Ivey and now he plays for the San Diego Padres."

"Is that so?" Was my only response as I got up to rejoin the team. I didn't have any time for small talk at that moment. The game started soon after that. Sometime, later during the game, I hit a ball so long that it sailed high over the fence to the top of the school building hitting the air conditioning unit. The momentum of my ball was traveling with such speed and force that it left a dent in the AC unit. After the game, I noticed old pops was still there. I couldn't help myself. I had to say something. I walked over and I said to him,

"Now you have seen two people hit that building: Mike Ivey from the San Diego Padres and Ron Smith from The Atlanta Cardinals."

I left McCoy Park a happy man that day.

THE CLOSER

Back in the sixties, while playing for the Atlanta Cardinals, I had never heard of the term closer in baseball. During those days, most pitchers in baseball, at every level, pitched nine innings. If the game tied and went into an extra inning or two or even three, pitchers were still expected to perform. That was their job. They were expected to do just that. Satchel Paige is the only pitcher I've ever known to pitch only two or three innings per game. That was during our barnstorming days with The Satchel Paige al-Stars.

Today, every team has what they call a closer; a pitcher who does not pitch during a regular game. He is only called upon, to take the mound, to shut down the opposing team in close games; thus, the name closer. His position is similar to that of the special team in the game of football.

Back in my Atlanta Cardinal days, Robert Mitchell was the go to pitcher who we depended upon in close games. When we were in tight games and needed to win, we called on Robert Mitchell or Mitch as we called him. That was his job. I have to laugh when I think about how terrible he was as a pitcher when we were in high school. We met on opposing baseball teams. I played for Archer High and he played for Howard High. We have shared a remarkable friendship through all these years. Back then, Mitch couldn't hit the side of a battleship with a handful of rice. It's amazing how he learned to control his pitches after being so wild in high school. For over twenty-five years he won many games for the Atlanta Cardinals. He was our closer long before this position became popular enough to use in the National Leagues.

Mitch and I devised a signal for him to secretly indicate to me when he was going to let the batter hit. He knew I could be depended on to catch any ball as long as it stayed in the ball park. I am amazed at the speed of my youthful legs. I could certainly use some of that youth and/or speed right now. That was his job. Over twenty-five years, a combination of my hitting and his pitching played a huge part in the success of the Atlanta Cardinals. After thinking about it, I would go so far as to say that Robert Mitchell, of the Atlanta Cardinals, was the first pitcher to hold the position of closer in the game of baseball. That's my opinion.

HAPEVILLE INCIDENT

The segregated South had its culture. It included strict rules for separating Blacks and Whites. If the rules were not followed, there were harsh consequences. Imagine trying to live under new rules which allowed the integration of Blacks and Whites. Change causes all types of reactions; anger, fear, delight, resistance, belief, hatred, displeasure, hope and pleasure. Plus, it takes time to adjust to change.

I was reminded of this while umpiring the tournament in Hapeville. My two partners and I were Black and working this all White baseball tournament. Integration was new and Black and White were doing their best to make it work while adapting to the change. The following is a case in point. There was a team from Forsyth County playing that day. At one point in the game, the coach's son called Frank Anthony, one of my fellow umpires, a Nigger. Frank had called him OUT and he disagreed with the call. We didn't know what to expect. Whatever happened next would set a precedent for the rest of the tournament. His father, the coach, immediately benched him for disrespecting the umpire. What a relief. Those kids would go far in life because they had a great coach. A good coach teaches not only skills for playing the game but also life skills. From then on, we could relax and do our job without any tension.

This was what it was going to take; working together for the good of mankind. We did such a good job in the tournament that we were offered the contract for the upcoming season. We had to decline because we had already accepted a contract for Gresham Park.

Baseball Scout Talent Search

During the process of trying to break into the Major Leagues, Blacks still had to contend with racism and the fact that teams maintained quotas. I heard the same story and/or excuse, whatever you want to call it, from scouts over and over again. They wanted to sign me but didn't have anywhere to send me.

While playing for The Atlanta Cardinals, I developed a few lasting relationships with baseball scouts. I was getting old, by baseball standards, at the age of twenty-three. In baseball, they want you to be at least eighteen; since, you're signed on projection. Teams are looking at the long term. First, you have to go to the Minor League for about three years. This leaves you ready for the draft at the age of twenty-one. However, I was still catching the eyes of several scouts. One of the scouts, Julian Morgan, and I hit it off at our first meeting. In fact, we later became friends. He scouted me and even took me to a few tryout camps. Disappointingly, the results were always the same with him, too. He would reluctantly relay the same words as the others. He wanted to sign me but he just didn't have anywhere to send me.

I knew of another player, Greg Harts, who I thought was pretty damn good. If I couldn't make it, I could at least try to help another player achieve success. With that thought in mind, I called Julian and asked him to come see him play. The team Greg played on was playing that Sunday against my team, The Cardinals. Would you believe he didn't play worth a damn? He was having a bad day. I couldn't believe it. Julian came to me, during the game, to inform me Greg had not impressed him. He didn't see what I saw in this guy. I was determined to get the scout to observe Greg at his finest. I approached Robert Mitchell, the Cardinals' pitcher, and asked him to let Greg hit so he would look good for the scout. He agreed and Greg continued to perform poorly.

After the game, Julian came to me with a mindset not to make a move on Greg. I used every persuasive tactic I could think of to convince him to give Greg a fair chance. He finally agreed with the understanding there would not be a big signing bonus. My efforts had paid off. Greg was going to have a chance at making it to the Majors. I imagine Greg received a few thousand dollars after signing. He was able to purchase new luggage and much needed clothing. I felt good because Julian Morgan had trusted my judgment. It was now up to Greg to make it to the draft.

Greg Harts received the call he had been waiting for in 1973 from the Mets. This was an exciting time for Greg. I can only imagine how he felt to be playing on the same team with the great Willie Mays. I remember how it was for me to play on the same team with the late, great Satchel Paige. That feeling of elation can be compared to a little child waking up on Christmas morning and finding the present he most desired under the tree. Greg didn't play long for the Mets but he made it to the show.

Cascade Park Controversy

Matthew Bell was assigned to umpire The Cardinals' game at Cascade Park. Bell had always managed teams that played against us. He was not one of our biggest fans even though he had once been a Cardinal, himself. He and I had a Gresham Park connection and we were friends.

The Cascade Park controversy arose out of a game where I hit a ball over a sixty feet high tree onto Cascade Road. To explain the situation; the tree was situated directly on the foul line. Half of the tree was in fair territory. The other half was in foul territory. The tree trunk was on the foul line. The ball, as seen by everyone there, was clearly a fair ball. No one had ever seen a ball hit that far in Cascade Park. Mr. Bell, the umpire, decided the ball was foul. After a long argument, his call stood.

After many, many years, Mr. Bell finally admitted that it was not a foul ball but a fair ball thereby making my hit a home run. This is what happened. Mr. Bell, a few other people from that era, and I attended the funeral of a friend. We piled into one car to pay our final respect at the cemetery. Our route coincidentally took us pass Cascade Park. Matthew Bell and I were sitting in the back. Mr. Bell, as he looked out the window, brought up that moment from the past. He chuckled and asked,

"Hey Ronnie, you remember that day you hit that ball and I said it was it was a foul?"

I had to smile, too. "Of course, I remember. Everybody remembers because you were wrong."

Sheepishly, he admitted, "I probably missed that one. But, yeah that was a homerun."

I laughed out loud. Everyone in the car laughed, too. We had all been Atlanta Cardinals at that time. This was history in the making. This admission was last year, the year 2012. It did make me feel a little better. That ball was one of the longest I had ever hit and I got nothing for it but a strike.

The Padres, A Veritable Sports Machine

One of my best moments in coaching was at Gresham Park while coaching my son when he was ten years old. He was playing on the eleven and twelve-year-old field with that age group. He was that talented and he also had the height and strength. Yes, he was large for his age.

We were scheduled to play what I thought was the best eleven and twelve- year-old team I had ever seen, The Padres. I still feel that way about them today. In my opinion, they were some of the best eleven and twelve-year-old athletes and the most talented players I'd had the privilege of seeing at that age. Others thought so, too and that's why the stands were always filled when The Padres played. It was exciting to watch this team play even though they were our opponent. The players on The Red Sox team were large for their age, also. Sadly, they weren't as athletic or talented as this team. This was going to be one of the best matchups of the season. Evidently, baseball fans from near and far thought so, too. The game between The Red Sox and The Padres drew one of the largest crowds I had ever seen at an eleven and twelve year olds game at Gresham Park.

The pitcher that I had planned to pitch against them had already told me, a few days before, leading up to the game, that his arm was sore. As his coach, I didn't believe his arm was hurting. He was probably experiencing a little fear in his heart, which I could understand. I didn't know what I was going to do since I didn't have a replacement pitcher. On my way to the park, the day of the game, I shared my thoughts with my son, Ron Smith Jr.,

"Well, I guess we will go and lose the game today."

My son had rarely heard me speak of defeat. He turned his head and pierced me with his eyes before asking,

"Why are we going to lose, Dad?" I thought a minute before revealing,

"We're going to lose because we don't have anybody to pitch today. Our pitcher called to let me know that his arm is hurting." He then asked me,

"What's wrong with me pitching today?"

My spirits lifted immediately but I didn't let him know that. I accepted his offer and let him know that was a good idea. I couldn't wait to get to Gresham Park. I hurried to make up the lineup.

The game started and The Padres looked very confident. I heard comments like; no ten year old can beat us. I was glad my son had volunteered because I wasn't a pushy dad/coach. I kept reminding myself of his age. I knew he was capable but I didn't know if he knew that about himself. Ron Jr. walked confidently to the mound with the knowledge that I would be signaling all the pitches for him to throw. My son was my best all-around player. He didn't play any particular position. He played wherever I put him. That way he learned to play each position and played it well. Okay, back to the game. When the game ended, my team, The Red Sox, won five to three. A lot of The Padres were crying. They weren't accustomed to losing. The Padres lost only two games that season. That was one day in my life that I will always cherish and I know my son feels the same. They lost to us, The Red Sox and to a team from Oklahoma in The World Series for their age group.

A large number of those boys, after finishing high school, went on to major colleges and did quite well.

Clemente Gordon went to Grambling University under a full football scholarship and played quarterback for four years. Mark Strickland, another player, played for The Atlanta Hawks and other teams as well. Bruno Williams attended Southern University on a full scholarship. Rodney Scott did well also. Mo Lewis received a full scholarship to The University of Georgia for football. After graduation, he went on to play linebacker for The New York Jets for more than ten years. As I stated previously, The Padres had a team full of not only athletic players but also talented players as well.

Moose, The Pitcher

A pitcher, who went by the name Moose, approached me at Forest Park where I was getting ready to umpire a game. It was the late 1980's. We exchanged the usual pleasantries and caught up on local news. While talking, Moose stated in a jovial tone,

"Hey man, I heard you used to be a good hitter." I smiled while answering, "Yeah man, I wasn't too bad." Out of the blue, he said,

"I bet you I can strike you out." I didn't know where this was coming from, but my reply to him was,

"Maybe you can but I doubt it."

Moose didn't know me at all. He had never even seen me play. He only knew what people had said about me. He only knew me as an umpire. He actually thought he was the greatest pitcher ever. At any rate, he was curious and wanted to prove I wasn't as good as people said I was.

I knew deep down inside that I hadn't played in over fifteen years since leaving The Cardinals. However, I felt pretty good. I was confident about being able to hit anything he threw at me. Moose was in his element because he told me to go get a bat. You know what? I didn't have anything to lose.

I looked around until I saw a member of one of the teams scheduled to play that day. After getting his attention, I asked him to throw me a bat. The player wanted to know what size. Shrugging my shoulders, I told him it really didn't matter; just choose one and throw it to me.

I caught the bat and didn't even check to see what size it was. Moose had challenged me in front of all these people and I was not going to let him get away with this. I have always loved a challenge. It gets my blood flowing and my adrenaline pumping.

As I approached the plate, Moose wanted to know if I was ready. He must have been feeling a little cocky by now. He had no idea how ready I was. If he had, I believe he would have stopped this madness right then. Oh well, let's have a little fun so I answered simply, yes I am. I hit the first and only pitch he threw over the center field fence. I don't have the slightest idea, to this day, how Moose felt but I felt pretty damn good.

I surprised myself. I remember thinking, ole Ron, you've still got it. All I wanted to do was make contact. I was confident I could hit the ball. But, I shocked myself when the ball went over the fence.

I couldn't believe, even though I hadn't played in fifteen years, I was still able to pull this off. Moose was the laughing stock of the ball park that day. He was teased all day long. It's a good thing Moose was a good-natured guy since people continued to tease him, in front of me, until he died a few years ago. I miss ole Moose.

Player/Manager

It was during the late seventies, while playing for The Atlanta Cardinals that I took over as manager when owner/manager, Sam Jones decided to step down. I was frequently asked if there was a conflict being both player and manager. Most of my team mates and I were around the same age. Plus, we had been playing as a team or as opponents since high school days. Because of my work ethic, I was a person who had the respect of most of the players.

There wasn't much opposition or discord within the team during the year I was manager. However, there were a few occasions when I had to demand respect. I remember one time we were playing a highly-contested game in Covington, Georgia. We were leading the game at the time. The other team had loaded the bases. My best friend's son, Ion, was the pitcher. I recognized the next hitter when he came up and I knew his weakness.

I immediately went to the mound. I told my pitcher what to throw to this particular hitter. He agreed and I came off the field. My pitcher decided to throw the pitch that he wanted to throw thereby blatantly ignoring my directive. The hitter hit a grand slam home run and we lost the game.

Anyone who knows me understands I do not like to lose. I was so damn mad at Ion. But, I quickly pulled myself together before saying anything to him because I didn't want to lose control. After the game was over, I approached Ion and said to him in a restrained voice, "Your father is my best friend but you can take off my uniform because you don't play for The Cardinals anymore." Without uttering a word, he pulled off the uniform and handed it to me.

This sounds cold and harsh; nevertheless, a player cannot play on my team if he ignores my instructions. Thirty-five years later, the son, the father and I are still friends. People used to ask me if it was difficult for me to kick him off the team. I always answered with an unhesitating and resounding NO.

Ron Smith

Coaching at Morehouse College

It was the year 1977. I remember it well. George Satterwhite, a former high school friend, surprised me with a call to ask if I could come to Morehouse College, an all-male HBCU, and help him coach the baseball team.

They were without a coach at that time. He was a Morehouse Man himself and wanted only the best for his team. He probably recalled the many sessions we had when he played for Archer High School.

I had graduated but went back to help him develop some skills and refine others. Needless to say, I accepted the offer. My brother (Ricky) was attending Morehouse on a baseball scholarship at the time and I knew several players.

These factors helped me make a quick decision. The team played extremely well and finished in second place to Florida A&M University, another HBCU in the SIAC Baseball Conference (Southern Intercollegiate Athletic Conference).

That was an outstanding accomplishment for this team. They brought pride and honor to their school. Morehouse was well known for its academia not its athleticism. One of the players from that team, Andre Patillo, is the current Athletic Director, a Morehouse Man. We continue to communicate with one another.

The Love of Baseball

The Atlanta Cardinals was an incredibly unique team. The manager, Frank Anthony, always wanted our appearance to be first class. He liked seeing us dressed in meticulous uniforms.

Frank also provided his team with good equipment. He wanted us to look like winners and we did. Each time we put on that Cardinals uniform, we stood a little straighter and held our heads a little higher. We were proud of our team. I guess that is how team spirit is formed. There were times Frank would order new uniforms with no way to pay for them. He never let a little thing like money stop the progress and success of this team.

There were players on the team who held down good jobs and didn't mind coming to Frank's rescue. We always came through to help Frank because he was using his own personal money for a team he not only admired but loved.

I remember one occasion where Frank ordered some new uniforms for a playoff game. He didn't have the money to get them out. The playoff was coming up that weekend. Frank came to me but I didn't have the money needed to get the uniforms out. I was working at a TV rental company at the time. I called Ted

Bowman, a teammate, and asked him to come and ride with me. We went out on my route and I collected enough money to go and get our uniforms out. Back in the day, when you bought an item on credit, you did not receive a bill in the mail. The bill collector came to your house to collect.

I used the money I had collected and made arrangements with my boss to pay it back later. My employer had a great appreciation for the game so he was okay with what I had done. That is what the love of baseball will make you do.

The Atlanta Cardinals vs The Braves

Another game comes to mind. I remember it really well. We, The Atlanta Cardinals, were playing The Braves, a team from the old Georgia Alabama League. They were our biggest rival. They came to Bankhead at Center Hill Park with the strong desire to beat us. We were ready.

The game was close and we were leading by one run in the last inning. The Braves had a runner on second with two outs. The batter got a hit to center field where I was playing. I charged the ball, fielded it on the run and made a perfect one bounce throw to our catcher. All he had to do was catch the ball and tag the runner out. However, he caught it and immediately dropped the ball and the game was tied. I was a little pissed as you can imagine. Well, we got the next out and left the field with a tied game.

I asked the team if they were ready to go home. I laid out a plan for ending this game. The plan was to get somebody on base. Since I was the fourth batter up that inning, I needed at least one person to reach base. Luckily, somebody did get on base which meant I would get a chance at bat. I don't remember how many pitches it took but I hit a home run and we went home victorious.

I went to a baseball showcase, January 18, 2014, in Peachtree City, Georgia. While I was there, taking in everything that was going on, I thought about the Martin Luther King, Jr Holiday and how it affected me.

It was a special moment for me as I looked around the field and stands. It came to me that neither the kids nor the parents in attendance knew how it used to be when attending a baseball game. Blacks and Whites wouldn't have been sitting together as we were that day. Blacks would have been relegated to the far end of the stands behind third base while the Whites would have been seated behind first base. Today, we can sit anywhere as long as we have the right ticket for that section.

Todays' young people don't see what I see when attending a sports event. Black and White kids did not play together on a team nor did they play against each other in competition as opponents. Everything was separate under the laws of segregation back in the forties and fifties during my youth.

I couldn't stop myself from thinking about the conditions I had to play under as a young boy. Black children didn't have a baseball field/diamond to play on. We played at the park, on vacant lots or in the field. We didn't have uniforms. We wore jeans and a white tee shirt. And, we certainly didn't have new up to date equipment. When White recreation centers received new equipment, their old, discarded and broken equipment was sent to us at the Black rec centers.

I wasn't able to prevent myself from staring appreciatively at the players out there on the field. They had all congregated here in Peachtree City, Georgia for the same purpose. They were a diverse group of young players, excited and hopeful about being seen by a college or professional scout. No one was marching and/or protesting this event. There weren't any threats of violence or hate groups trying to keep these kids separated because of their skin color or their race.

The young people of today don't have the slightest idea of how blessed they are to be able to come together in peace and harmony, while participating in a showcase being held at a real stadium with a baseball diamond.

While in this reflective mood, I thought about the time, in the 60's, when I went to Ponce de Leon Park to try out for an NBL team. All Blacks were turned away by the scouts and told to meet them later that evening at Mosley Park. You see, Mosley Park was a park for Blacks. We couldn't try out at Ponce de Leon Park because that was a park for Whites.

You can't imagine how I felt; angry, frustrated, annoyed and upset. This is one reason why I feel we should all observe the King Holiday and try to learn as much about our past as possible. We should not be taking the way we live for granted since so many people, Black and White, shed their blood and died fighting for the civil rights of all.

HERITAGE WEEK CELEBRATION

The Atlanta Braves second annual Heritage Weekend was held at Turner Field Friday, May 2 through Sunday, May 4, 2014. The Braves hosted a weekend of events to honor baseball's role in affecting social change and to celebrate Atlanta's culturally rich diversity.

Saturday, May 3, 2014 was the Heritage Game. The Braves honored former Negro League players by wearing the uniform of the Atlanta Black Crackers while the opposing team honored the Negro League players by wearing the San Francisco Sea Lions uniform. Saturday night's Heritage Game began with a special tribute to the Negro League. This included a pregame autograph session featuring 25 former Negro League players. I can proudly say that I was included in that group. Imagine that! There I was being treated like an all-star with people standing in line to get my autograph......Me, Ronald Smith. This was conducted in a holding area before going out on the field to be presented to the world. Many of the players were in their 80's and 90's. I was one of the few younger players at seventy-one. All of us were happy and surprised at being asked to participate. However, I could barely retain my excitement when we lined up and walked out on that field. The crowd went wild with enthusiasm as each one of us stepped out onto the field. I thought my heart was going to burst with pride and appreciation. My heart was pounding as loud as the cheers. As I looked around and saw all those fans standing, yelling, whistling and clapping for us (for me), tears formed behind my eyes. They didn't fall but I knew they were there. I had been waiting for so long for my talent and participation in the baseball world to be recognized and here it was. I just stood in the moment and breathed it all in. Man, that was a good feeling. After we lined up on the field, our names were called one by one and the camera zoomed in on us and put our face on the jumbo screen with our name. There I was, for the world to see, on the jumbo screen. I will never forget that one moment in time.

I got a chance to see a lot of the old players from the past some I knew and some I had only heard of. Included in that group was 96-year-old legend James "Red" Moore of the Atlanta Black Crackers, Larry Williams of the Kansas City

Monarchs and Ernest "Big Dog" Fan of the Birmingham Black Barons. Ninety-five- year-old, Roosevelt Jackson, of the Miami Red Sox, couldn't contain himself during the announcements. He broke away from the group and started dancing. He kicked his legs, waved his arms and busted a few moves before he was gently escorted back to the lineup. I was shocked to learn Mr. Jackson is completely blind! I know he had a good time. I cannot say enough about the staff.

I have my invitation as a memento of this occasion. It was one of the most enjoyable events that I have ever been a part of. We were treated as royalty by the Braves organization. We received a special parking pass for the occasion. Upon arriving, wheelchair, and golf cart services were waiting for those who needed them. Anyone who knows me would not be surprised that I walked from the parking lot to the banquet hall where we gathered for meet and greet. My passion is food services and my eyes lit up when I saw the spread they had prepared for us; beef briskets, jumbo shrimp, fruit and vegetable trays, desserts, salads, crab legs, potatoes, rice, green beans, etc. That wasn't all. That's just what I remembered. There was so much food; I didn't know where to begin. So, I sampled a little bit of just about everything. Whatever your drinking preference, it was there for the taking and/or asking.

The fans at the game really received us well. Their response made me feel appreciated. After our stint on the field, we returned to a master viewing suite to watch the game between The Braves and The San Francisco Giants. There was another feast waiting for us with a completely different menu. This time it was every pasta you could name, chicken wings, all types of dip, cole slaw, and other finger foods. Name a drink or a beverage and it was prepared for you. We were given a reception fit for a king. The food was marvelous and the service was excellent. I enjoyed the game even though The Braves lost to San Francisco 4-1. Oh well, there's always tomorrow.

After the game, I left. I did not remain for the free Celebration Concert by Kool and the Gang. This time I accepted the offer of the golf cart service back to my car. It had been a long day and I must admit; I was tired. This is a day that I will always remember as long as I live. I have always had pessimistic feelings about the way major league baseball treats Black players. After my experience at Turner Field, during The Braves second annual Heritage Weekend, I'm prepared to let go of a lot of negative feelings and resentment. I sincerely appreciated the treatment I received from The Braves and their staff during their 2014 Heritage Weekend.

Made in the USA
Columbia, SC
21 August 2024